The Lighthouse Companion
for
Massachusetts, Rhode Island, and New Hampshire

Photographs by Paul Rezendes

Published by Tide-mark Press
Windsor, Connecticut

Copyright 2004 by Paul Rezendes and Tide-mark Press

Published by Tide-mark Press Ltd.
P.O. Box 20, Windsor, CT 06095

Printed in Korea by Samhwa Printing Co.

Design and typography by Paul Rasid

Special thanks to Lorraine Alexson
for her work on this manuscript

Library of Congress Control Number: 2003113657

ISBN 1-55949-878-1

First Edition

Table of Contents

Fort Pickering Light is located on a rocky piece of real estate in Salem Harbor called Winter Island.

Lighthouses have played a long and important role in Massachusetts's history since the days of colonization. The state's first light, Boston Light, is the nation's oldest U.S. light station, established in 1716. Over the years, Boston Light was joined by more than 60 other beacons, though not all of those are currently active. The lighthouses of Massachusetts are distinct in that they represent a wide variety of architectural styles within a relatively short driving distance. This is one destination that true lighthouse lovers should not miss!

Also included in this chapter are the lighthouses of New Hampshire. A small state with a minimum of coastline, there are only two active lighthouses in the "Granite State," the Isles of Shoals Light and Portsmouth Harbor Light. These lighthouses are integrated alphabetically with the Massachusetts lights on the following pages.

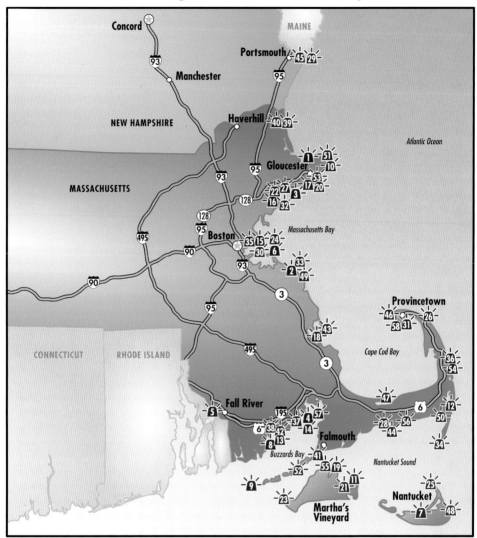

Lighthouse Number	Lighthouse Name	Page
1	Annisquam Harbor Light	8
2	Antoine and Wilson Memorial	10
3	Bakers Island Light	12
4	Bird Island Light	14
5	Borden Flats Light	16
6	Boston Light	18
7	Brant Point Light	20
8	Butler Flats Light	22
9	Buzzards Bay Entrance Tower	24
10	Cape Ann Light Station on Thacher Island	26
11	Cape Pogue Light	28

Lighthouse Number	Lighthouse Name	Page

Annisquam Harbor Light

Latitude: 42° 39' 42" N
Longitude: 70° 40' 54" W

Contact Information:
First U.S. Coast Guard District
408 Atlantic Avenue
Boston, Massachusetts 02210-3350
(617) 223-8243

Lodged at the entrance to Annisquam Harbor is the oldest of the four lighthouse stations ringing the Gloucester peninsula. The first beacon was built at Wigwam Point in 1801 to keep seafarers clear of the dangerous Squam Bar. Land for a 32-foot wooden tower and keeper's house was purchased at that time from Massachusetts for $140.

In service for 50 years, the original tower was replaced with a new 40-foot octagonal one in 1851. Five years later, it received a new, fifth-order Fresnel lens rotated with a clockwork mechanism.

Annisquam Harbor Light

Annisquam, Massachusetts

Directions:
Take Route 128 north into Gloucester. At the rotary, exit at 9 o'clock, Route 127 (Washington Street). Follow Route 127 (Washington Street) to Bridgewater Street. Take a left onto Bridgewater Street. Follow to Leonard Street. Take a right onto Leonard Street. Follow to Norrock Road. Take a left onto Norrock Road. Follow to Ocean Avenue. Take a left onto Ocean Avenue. Follow to Norwood Heights. Take a left onto Norwood Heights. Follow Norwood Heights to Wigwam Road. Take a left onto Wigwam Road. Follow to Lighthouse Road. Take a right onto Lighthouse Road. Follow Lighthouse Road to Norwood Heights (again). Take a left onto Norwood Heights. There is a small parking area near the lighthouse.

As the century wound down, that wooden tower was supplanted in 1897 with the current 41-foot brick tower constructed on a stone foundation. About that time, the station had a notable guest, Rudyard Kipling, who wrote *Captain's Courageous* while staying at the keeper's house. In 1922, electricity came to the station, and the light's fifth-order Fresnel lens and kerosene-powered lamp were swapped for an electrified fourth-order Fresnel lens. The move boosted the beacon's brilliance from 1,300 to 250,000 candlepower. Automated in 1974, today the signal has a 190-millimeter plastic optic, which was installed in 1988. The light flashes white 45 feet above sea level every 7.5 seconds and has a red sector from 180 to 217 degrees. A major renovation of the tower was completed in 2000. Although modified over the years, the original keeper's house remains at the site occupied by a U.S. Coast Guard family.

Antoine and Wilson Memorial

Latitude: N/A
Longitude: N/A

Contact Information:
Cohasset Lightkeepers' Corporation (CLC)
P.O. Box 514
Cohasset, Massachusetts 02025
(781) 383-1433

Nearly 150 years after their deaths, Joseph Antoine and Joseph Wilson received recognition for making the ultimate sacrifice on April 16, 1851.

Antoine and Wilson Memorial

Cohasset, Massachusetts

Directions:
The keeper's quarters, fog bell, and a replica of the lantern room that houses part of the original Fresnel lens from Minot's Ledge Light can be seen at Government Island in Cohasset. Take Route 3A into Cohasset to Route 228. Follow Route 228 north to East Street. Follow East Street. It will become North Main Street. North Main Street becomes South Main Street. Follow South Main Street to Summer Street and turn left. Follow Summer Street to Border Street. Take a right at Border Street. After crossing a bridge, take an immediate left onto Government Island.

Antoine and Wilson were assistant keepers at the first lighthouse built at Minot's Ledge, just south of Boston harbor. The structure, which looked like a giant iron spider clinging to the ledge's crags, had been criticized since its inception for its instability.

On April 11, the light's keeper went ashore, leaving the lighthouse's operation in the able hands of his assistants. He never returned to the station. A furious nor'easter moved in and raged for days on end. Then, on the night of April 16, locals on the mainland were awakened by the unremitting clanging of the light's fog bell.

When daylight broke, the spider light was gone, razed by storm and sea. The bodies of the assistants were recovered later. Wilson swam to a nearby island, where it is believed he died of exhaustion and exposure. Antoine's body washed ashore at Nantasket. According to local legend, during tempestuous weather, sailors have heard wails emanating from Minot's Ledge that sound like Portuguese, Antoine's native tongue, for "Stay away! Stay away!"

A granite monument memorializing Antoine and Wilson was dedicated on May 21, 2000. It is located on Government Island in Cohasset, where the keeper's house has been restored and the beacon's lantern room reconstructed.

Bakers Island Light

Latitude: 42° 32' 12" N
Longitude: 70° 47' 12" W

Contact Information:
First U.S. Coast Guard District
408 Atlantic Avenue
Boston, Massachusetts 02210-3350
(617) 223-8243

Fifty-five-acre Bakers Island, located 6 miles east of Salem and 3 miles northeast of Marblehead Neck, is the largest residential isle north of Boston. It is part of a 15-island chain known as The Miseries, the scene of many shipwrecks over the centuries. Appropriately enough, legend has it that Bakers itself was named after a visitor to the island who was killed by a falling tree.

Bakers Island Light

Salem, Massachusetts

Directions:
The light is closed to the public and is best
seen by boat. However, a distant view of the
lighthouse is possible from the Harbor Street–
Boardman Avenue loop off Highway 127 in
Manchester-by-the-Sea; from Winter Island
Park in Salem; and from Chandler Hovey Park
on Marblehead Neck. Excursion providers
include Boston Harbor Cruises, One Long
Wharf, Boston, Massachusetts 02110;
(617) 227-4321 or (877) 733-9425.

After three ships sank near the island in 1796,
costing 16 men their lives, Congress appropriated
$6,000 for twin lights to be built at the site. A
two-story keeper's house was constructed, and
twin beacons, first lighted in 1798, were placed
40 feet apart at each end of the building.

When one of the lights became disabled in 1816, mariners complained that
the Bakers station could be easily confused with Boston Light. Their complaints proved prescient as nautical mishaps multiplied with only a single
signal to guide seafarers in the area. In 1820, two new tower lights were
built at the site. Since one tower was taller than the other, the lights became
known as the Mr. and Mrs. lighthouses. A one-and-a-half-story Victorian
keeper's house was added to the station in 1828.

In 1926, the smaller of the two towers was removed. The remaining light is a
59-foot conical white granite beacon. It was fitted with a fourth-order Fresnel
lens in 1855, which has been replaced with a VRB-25 190-millimeter plastic
optic. It flashes 111 feet above sea level alternately red and white every 20
seconds. Its foghorn emits a 3-second blast every 30 seconds.

The light was electrified in 1938 and automated in 1972. Major renovations
were made in 1993 and 1996, and the light became solar-powered in 2000.

Bird Island Light

Latitude: 41° 40' 10" N
Longitude: 70° 43' 02" W

Contact Information:
Bird Island Preservation Society
2 Spring Street
Marion, Massachusetts 02738
(508) 748-0550
Website: by-the-sea.com/birdislandlight/

Because of their isolation, some lighthouses felt like prison for their keepers and Bird Island Light may have been an actual jail for its first helmsman. According to local lore, William S. Moore was banished to the light, built in 1819, for his swashbuckling ways. Conjugal visits were not a problem for

Bird Island Light

Marion, Massachusetts

Directions:
From New Bedford take Interstate 195 north to exit 20. At the end of the ramp turn right onto Route 105 (Front Street). Stay on Route 105 for 0.7 mile and turn left onto Route 6 (Wareham Street). Take Route 6 for 0.7 mile, then bear right onto Creek Road. Go 0.5 mile on Creek Road to the end and take a right onto Point Road. Follow Point Road 4.1 miles to the end at the golf course. The lighthouse can be seen in the distance from along the seawall.

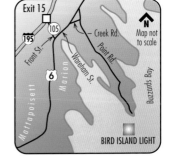

him, though. The authorities permitted his wife to live with him on the island. Moore's missus died on the cay, which is less than two acres in size and located a few hundred yards off Butlers Point in Sippican Harbor by Marion, Massachusetts. Some say Moore killed her. Moore said she died from some bad tobacco. Death apparently did not give her everlasting peace, however, as her spirit has been heard over the years rapping late at night on the door to the keeper's house.

The light, a 31-foot-tall, white rubblestone cone with a focal plane of 37 feet, was one of only a few in its early days to have a revolving optic. Around 1852, its original optic—10 lamps with 14-inch reflectors—was replaced with a fourth-order Fresnel lens, which was later supplanted in 1997 with a solar-powered lantern with an acrylic lens.

Although the opening of Cape Cod Canal in 1914 increased traffic through Buzzards Bay, a series of buoys near the main shipping channels nixed the need for the light, and it was decommissioned in 1933. In 1940, the island, now an important nesting site for common and roseate terns, was sold to a private party. It became the property of Marion in 1966. The light was briefly relighted in 1976, but it was not until 1997 that it was relighted permanently as a fully automated private aid to navigation.

Borden Flats Light

Latitude: 41° 42' 18" N
Longitude: 71° 10' 30" W

Contact Information:
Fall River Historical Society
451 Rock Street
Fall River, Massachusetts 02720
(508) 679-1071
Website: www.lizzieborden.org

Borden Flats Light

Fall River, Massachusetts

Directions:
Take Interstate 195 to Fall River. Take the exit for Route 138 south (Broadway). Stay on Route 138 for 0.6 mile then take a right onto William Street. Take William Street for 0.2 mile, and take a right onto Almond Street. Follow to the road's end, then turn left into the Borden Light Marina's free parking lot. The lighthouse can be seen to the west of the marina.

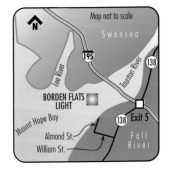

Bearing the name of the family that spawned a notorious Victorian parenticide, Borden Flats Light sits like a gigantic alabaster sparkplug at the mouth of the Taunton River in Mount Hope Bay. On June 16, 1880, $25,000 was appropriated to build the 50-foot edifice, which replaced an unlighted day beacon used to mark a reef at the river's end. The light was named after longtime residents of Fall River, the prominent Borden family, whose most infamous member, Lizzie Borden, was charged and acquitted of axing her parents in 1893.

The light rests on a cylindrical cast-iron caisson filled with concrete and sunk into a reef. Builders erected a cast-iron tower on top of the caisson. After the devastating Hurricane of 1938 damaged the light, a wider caisson was built around the original. Rainwater was collected in the structure's gutters and deposited in a cistern at the base of the building. Five stories rise above the cistern. Two were used by the crew that staffed the light before it was fully automated in 1963.

The original light had a fog bell operated by machinery and a state-of-the-art fourth-order Fresnel lens. Borden Flats Light was electrified in 1957, and its Fresnel lens replaced with a plastic one in 1977. Its fog bell remained in use until 1983, when it was replaced with an electric foghorn. The light, which flashes white every 2.5 seconds, remains an active U.S. Coast Guard aid to navigation.

Boston Light

Latitude: 42° 19' 42" N
Longitude: 70° 53' 24" W

Contact Information:
The Friends of the Boston Harbor Islands
P.O. Box 690187
Quincy, Massachusetts 02269-0187
(781) 740-4290
E-mail: fbhi@earthlink.net Website: www.fbhi.org/

Built in 1716, Boston Light was the first lighthouse erected in North America. Located on Little Brewster Island in Boston Harbor, the operation of the first stone lighthouse at the site was financed by taxing shipping through the harbor at the rate of a penny per ton.

In 1719, America's first fog signal was created on the island: a cannon, which has been preserved and sits today at the foot of the latest light.

Boston Light

Boston, Massachusetts

Directions:
Boston Light is accessible only by boat. The Friends of the Boston Harbor Islands and the Boston Island Partnership sponsor trips to the light during the summer. Information and reservations can be obtained by calling (617) 223-8666.

During the Revolutionary War, the beacon was destroyed three times. Early in July 1775, colonial troops set the signal's wooden parts on fire, but the British immediately began repairing the structure. That forced another raid by the Americans. The following year, the Lobsterbacks, no longer able to hold the Hub, retreated and demolished the signal with explosives.

After the war, in 1783, a 75-foot rubblestone tower was raised at the site. The structure is the country's second oldest after New Jersey's Sandy Hook Light, built in 1764. A number of improvements were made to the structure in 1859. The tower was extended to 89 feet. A second-order Fresnel lens, which revolved by a wind-up mechanism, was added. The tower was strengthened with a brick liner and a duplex keeper's house constructed.

In 1884, a cistern was built that could hold up to 21,800 gallons of rainwater. A year later, a second keeper's house was constructed. In its heyday, three keepers and their families inhabited the island. During World War II, the beacon was extinguished for security reasons. Later in the 1940s, the lighthouse was electrified, and the mechanical works for its Fresnel, still used today and whose white flash can be seen for a distance of 27 miles, was supplanted with an electric motor.

In 1998, Boston Light became the last lighthouse in the United States to be automated. However, a U.S. Coast Guard crew, which performs most of the traditional duties of their forebears, is still stationed on the island.

Brant Point Light

Latitude: 41° 17' 24" N
Longitude: 70° 05' 30" W

Contact Information:
U.S. Coast Guard Station
Brant Point, Nantucket
(508) 228-0398

Brant Point Light

Nantucket, Massachusetts

Directions:
From ferry landing, follow Broad Street to South Beach Street. Turn right on South Beach Street. Follow to Easton Street and turn right. The lighthouse is at the end of the street.

Brant Point's first beacon, established in 1746, was the second lighthouse built in the United States, after Boston Light in 1716. Since that time, 10 lighthouses have occupied the area on the western side of Nantucket Harbor. The first five lights were no more than lanterns on platforms with varying degrees of effectiveness. The fourth light, for instance, was so dim, sailors said it looked like a firefly at night. Salty wags dubbed it the "bug light." All five lighthouses were destroyed by fire or storm from 1758 to 1788.

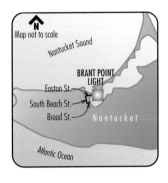

The sixth lighthouse, controlled by the federal government since 1795, was condemned in 1825 and replaced for $1,600 with a tower erected on the roof of the keeper's house. By 1854, the seventh light showed signs of serious deterioration. Congress appropriated $15,000 to build a new signal and keeper's house at the Point. Construction of those brick dwellings was completed in 1856. The light was housed in a 47-foot tower with a fourth-order Fresnel lens. That light became obsolete in 1900, and its functions were assumed by a fixed red light on a pole. The tenth and current conical light was erected in 1901. Built of wood and 26 feet tall (the lowest in New England), it had a fifth-order Fresnel visible for 10 nautical miles. Its white beam was changed to red in 1933 to avoid confusion with lights from surrounding buildings. That lens was replaced with a 250-millimeter optic, which emits a red light flashing every four seconds. Full automation came to the light in 1965. Still standing in the general area are the 1856 tower without a lantern room, a keeper's house (1856), two wooden range light towers (1908), an oil house (1904), a storage building (1901), a garage (1901), a lifesaving station (1934), and a boathouse (1936).

Butler Flats Light

Latitude: 41° 36' 12" N
Longitude: 70° 53' 42" W

Contact Information:
City of New Bedford
133 William Street
New Bedford, Massachusetts 02740
Website: www.ci.new-bedford.ma.us

The whaling industry had long fizzled when Butler Flats Light was fired up in 1898, but New Bedford, known as the Whaling City, remained an industrial powerhouse. As the third largest manufacturing city in the Bay State, more than 500,000 tons of shipping entered the port in 1890 alone. Built for $34,000, the beacon—situated in New Bedford Channel at the mouth of the Acushnet River—replaced Clark's Point Light, whose illumination

Directions:
Take Interstate 195 into New Bedford. Take exit 15 for Route 18 south. Stay on Route 18 for 2.5 miles, then take a left onto Cove Street. Take Cove Street for 0.4 mile and turn right onto East Rodney French Boulevard. Go about 1.3 miles to the intersection with Ricketson Street. You can view the lighthouse from along the seawall. A sea view of the light can be gained by taking a ride on the Martha's Vineyard ferry, which leaves from Billy Woods Wharf on East Rodney French Boulevard, or the Cuttyhunk ferry, which leaves from Pier 3/Fisherman's Wharf.

works had been relocated in 1869 to Fort Tabor, later renamed Fort Rodman. The new light was the handiwork of F. Hopkinson Smith, an artist and writer who had designed Race Rock Light at the entrance to Long Island Sound and built the foundation for the Statue of Liberty.

With no solid rock for a foundation, Butler Flats Light presented its builders with some challenges. After dredging 5 feet of mud from the bottom of the channel, a 35-foot iron cylinder was lowered into the muck and filled with stone and concrete. A 53-foot brick sparkplug-style lighthouse was built on top of the cylinder. The edifice contains such interesting architectural details as brick windowsills, raised brick below the watchroom deck, and quasi-Italian, cast-iron brackets supporting the lantern gallery.

After a new automatic light and fog signal were built on the city's hurricane barrier in 1975, the U.S. Coast Guard found the navigational aid unnecessary. In 1978, New Bedford gained control of the structure and fully automated the light, replacing its kerosene-powered fifth-order Fresnel lens with solar-powered optics. The light had another optical upgrade in 1998 with the installation of a Tidelands RB-300 MaxLumina locating beacon.

Buzzards Bay Entrance Tower

Buzzards Bay Entrance Tower

Buzzards Bay, Massachusetts

Directions:
There is no public access to the light. It is best seen by private boat.

Looking more like an oil rig than a lighthouse, the original Buzzards Bay Entrance Tower was built in 1961. Steel pilings filled with concrete formed the foundation for this "Texas Tower"-style platform. Originally equipped with a DCB-224 optic, the station was automated in 1980 and deactivated in 1994. The current entrance light was erected in 1997. Standing on three legs with a large central column, all painted red, the platform stands 67 feet above sea level. Its light flashes white every 2.5 seconds, and during periods of low visibility its foghorn sounds two blasts every 30 seconds. A helicopter landing pad and automated weather station can be found at the light.

Latitude: 41° 23' 48" N
Longitude: 71° 02' 01" W

Contact Information:
First U.S. Coast Guard District
408 Atlantic Avenue
Boston, Massachusetts 02210-3350
(617) 223-8243

Cape Ann Light Station on Thacher Island

Contact Information:
Thacher Island Town Committee
P.O. Box 73
Rockport, Massachusetts 01966
(978) 546-7697
E-mail: info@thacherisland.org
Website: www.thacherisland.org

North Light:
Latitude: 42° 38' 24" N
Longitude: 70° 34' 30" W

South Light:
Latitude: 42° 38' 12" N
Longitude: 70° 34' 30" W

Named after a survivor of a 1635 shipwreck, 50-acre Thacher Island, three-quarters of a mile off Rockport, Massachusetts, received its first brace of lights in 1771, making it the last station constructed under British rule. Up to that time, the colonials built light stations only to mark the entrance to harbors. The Cape Ann twins were the first lighthouse raised to warn seafarers of a marine hazard, Londoner Ledge, located southeast of the key. Shortly following initial ignition, the 45-foot stone beacons went dark as a group of Minutemen forced the Tory keeper of the lighthouse to flee his station. They remained so until the end of the Revolutionary War.

Cape Ann Light Station on Thacher Island

Rockport, Massachusetts

Directions:
Follow U.S. Route 95 north to Route 128.
Follow Route 128 to Route 127A. Follow Route
127A to South Street in Rockport. Follow South
Street to Penryn Way. Follow Penryn Way to
Penzance Road. Follow Penzance Road to shore.
The lights are visible from the shore. Cruises
offered by excursion companies can give you
great views of the lights from the water.

You can also join the Thacher Island Association
and take advantage of its shuttles to the island in
July and August from 9:00 to 11:00 A.M. For
reservations, call (978) 546-7697. The athleti-
cally inclined can rent kayaks at the North Shore
Kayak Outdoor Center (978-546-5050) and
paddle out to the island. Information on camping
and lodging on the island is available at
www.thacherisland.org.

After more than 80 years of service, the original signals were replaced in
1861 with two 124-foot conical granite towers equipped with first-order
Fresnel lenses costing $10,000 each.

Electricity came to the island in 1932 by way of a 6,000-foot submarine
cable. At that time the northern tower was decommissioned. Automated in
1979, the southeast light flashes its 70,000-candlepower, 200-millimeter,
VRB-25, solar-powered, red light every 5 seconds. It can be seen for a
distance of 19 miles. In 1988, thanks to the efforts of the Thacher Island
Association, the north tower was relighted, and its fixed yellow light now
serves as a private aid to navigation. Buildings still standing on the island
include the keeper's house, the assistant keeper's house, the fog signal
building, a boathouse, and an oil house.

Cape Pogue Light

Latitude: 41° 25' 12" N
Longitude: 70° 27' 12" W

Contact Information:
Cape Pogue Wildlife Refuge
(508) 627-7689
E-mail: islands@ttor.org

Cape Pogue Light

Edgartown (Martha's Vineyard), Massachusetts

Directions:
Take the ferry from Edgartown to
Chappaquiddick. From the ferry landing, take
Chappaquiddick Road for about 2.5 miles. At
a sharp right curve, continue straight onto
Dike Road, a dirt road, for 0.5 mile to Dike
Bridge. Drive over Dike Bridge to the Cape
Pogue gatehouse and entrance. Cape Pogue
Light is a 3.5-mile hike from the Cape Pogue
gatehouse. Tours of the light are also offered
by Cape Pogue Wildlife Refuge.

The lighthouses at Cape Pogue have had to be
vagabonds to evade the sea's embrace. Located
on a bluff at the northeast point of
Chappaquiddick Island, the first light at the
Cape was raised in 1802. A 35-foot wooden
tower built for $2,000, it shone a fixed white
light 55 feet above sea level. To escape encroaching erosion, the beacon was
moved farther inland in 1838. By 1844, the tower had reached such a state
of disrepair that it had to be replaced with a new, 33-foot octagonal wooden
structure and a larger keeper's house. In 1857, the light's lens was upgraded
to a fourth-order Fresnel. The ocean continued to threaten the site, and in
1893 a "temporary" 35-foot conical tower with white wooden shingles was
constructed 40 feet from the 1844 light. That temporary light remains on
the site today and has been moved four times since 1907.

Full automation came to the lighthouse in 1943, and the keeper's house was
demolished in 1954. During its last move in 1987, when the sentinel was 13
feet from sliding into the brine, a Sikorsky Skycrane helicopter moved the
light 500 feet inland. At that time, the signal was refitted with a 300-milli-
meter solar-powered lens that flashes white every 6 seconds 65 feet above sea
level. The old Fresnel lens is on display at the Martha's Vineyard Historical
Society Museum in Edgartown. The lighthouse at Cape Pogue is one of the
few wooden lighthouses remaining in the world.

Chatham Light

Latitude: 41° 40' 18" N
Longitude: 69° 57' 00" W

Contact Information:
U.S. Coast Guard
(508) 945-3830
U.S. Coast Guard Auxiliary
(508) 430-0628

Seafarers have long looked to the lights at Chatham to navigate the dicey waters enveloping the "elbow" of Cape Cod. The first beacons at the location were built in 1808. They were two 40-foot wooden towers situated 70 feet apart on James Head, a 50-foot bluff near the entrance to Chatham Harbor. Wind and weather undermined the structural integrity of the towers by 1841, and two new 40-foot brick towers were raised farther inland on the head. They had nine lamps, fueled by whale oil, with 14-inch reflectors and displayed fixed white beams. In 1857, both lights were refitted with fourth-order Fresnel lenses.

A vicious nor'easter in 1870 altered the erosion pattern in the area and by 1877 the beacons, originally 228 feet from the bluff's edge, found themselves a mere 48 feet from oblivion. Yet another pair of signals, as

Chatham, Massachusetts

Directions:

Take Massachusetts Route 3 south (Southeast
Expressway) to Route 6. Follow Route 6 over the
Sagamore Bridge to exit 11. Follow exit 11 to
Route 137. Follow Route 137 toward Brewster
and Chatham to Old Queen Anne Road. Turn left
on Old Queen Anne Road and follow to Main
Street (Route 28). Turn left onto Main Street and
follow to Shore Road. At the intersection with
Shore Road, turn right to remain on Main Street.
Follow Main Street to the lighthouse.

well as a one-and-a-half-story keeper's house,
were erected at the site. Each 48 feet high, the
conical, brick-lined, cast-iron towers were built
100 feet apart and fitted with the lenses from the
old lighthouses.

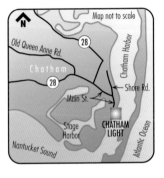

With the digging of the Cape Cod canal, traffic around the peninsula
slackened, and in 1923, the twins were separated. The south tower was
moved to Nauset Beach in North Eastham, Massachusetts. Meanwhile, the
U.S. Coast Guard upgraded the north tower's lens to a rotating fourth-
order Fresnel illuminated by a 30,000 candlepower incandescent oil vapor
lamp, which emitted four white flashes every 30 seconds at 80 feet above
sea level. When the beacon was electrified in 1939, that lamp was swapped
for an electric one with an intensity of 800,000 candlepower.

The light's lantern room was removed and rebuilt in 1969. The Fresnel
(now on exhibit at the Chatham Historical Society) was supplanted with
2.8 million candlepower rotating Aerobeacons that flash white twice every
10 seconds and are visible for 24 nautical miles. In 1982, the lighthouse
was automated, and in 1993, a new Aerobeacon DCB-224 optic was
installed. The U.S. Coast Guard Auxiliary Flotilla 1101 adopted the light
in 1994. The group schedules tours of the beacon throughout the year.

Clark's Point Light with Butler Flats Light in the distance.

Latitude: 41° 35' 35" N
Longitude: 70° 54' 04" W

Contact Information:
City of New Bedford
133 William Street
New Bedford, Massachusetts 02740
Website: www.ci.new-bedford.ma.us/

Clark's Point Light stands at the southern entrance to New Bedford Harbor. The need for a navigational aid at the site was recognized in 1797 when local merchants raised a wooden beacon to guide ships from Buzzards Bay into the entrepôt. It did not take long for maritime authorities to realize the necessity for a more permanent structure, and in 1804, a 42-foot stone tower was erected at the location. In celebration of the achievement, workers were treated to a 100-gallon pot of chowder.

Clark's Point Light

New Bedford, Massachusetts

Directions:
The lighthouse is not open to the public, but the grounds around it are a public park. To reach the lighthouse, take U.S. Route 195 to exit 15, Route 18. Take Route 18 south to Cove Street. Take a left onto Cove Street. Follow Cove Street to Rodney French Boulevard. Follow Rodney French Boulevard to Brock Avenue. Take a left onto Brock Avenue. Follow Brock Avenue to South Rodney French Boulevard. Take a left onto South Rodney French Boulevard. Follow South Rodney French Boulevard to the parking area to park.

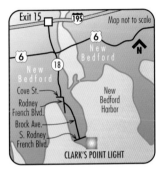

During the era of Civil War hysteria, Fort Tabor, a seven-sided bastion intended to protect the "Whaling City" from Confederate raiders, was built close to the lighthouse—so close that it obscured the light's beacon. So in 1869, the station's lantern room and keeper's quarters were relocated to a short, stout structure atop the fort, where it remains today. The old tower was left unattended until it was demolished in 1906.

When Butler Flats Light was constructed in 1898, Clark's Light was decommissioned. The light and fort, renamed Fort Rodman, were forsaken for decades. Then, in the 1970s, efforts were made to restore the buildings, only to be thwarted by vandals and thieves. A second and more ambitious restoration effort was launched in 1997. It called for $7 million to be spent on sprucing up the light and fort and turning the adjacent area into a public park with biking and walking paths, a boathouse, a bathhouse, and a community center. At the turn of the 21st century, revitalization work went into high gear, and in 2001 the lighthouse was relighted on its 132nd anniversary.

Cleveland East Ledge Light

Latitude: 41° 37' 54" N
Longitude: 70° 41' 42" W

Contact Information:
First Coast Guard District
408 Atlantic Avenue
Boston, Massachusetts 02210-3350
(617) 223-8243

Cleveland East Ledge Light

Bourne, Massachusetts

Directions:
From the rotary at the Bourne Bridge, take
Route 28 south. Bear right onto Route 28A.
Follow 28A to Wing Road. Take a right on
Wing Road to Quaker Road. Take a left on
Quaker Road to Old Silver Beach. Make sure to
take your binoculars with you.

From Bauhaus to the lighthouse is the route
taken by the builders of the Cleveland East Ledge
Light on Buzzards Bay near Pocasset, a village of
Bourne, Massachusetts. Departing from traditional "sparkplug" designs, architects created in
1943 a distinctive Art Moderne lighthouse with a
70-foot conical tower emerging from a square
dwelling, which served as the keeper's quarters

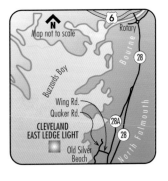

until the light was fully automated in 1978. The white obelisk, which has a
focal plane of 74 feet, is built of reinforced concrete. Tower and dwelling
rest on a rust-brown stone and concrete caisson.

The tower's original lens was a fourth-order Fresnel, which was replaced in
1978 with a 190-millimeter lens. Its light pattern is a flashing white every
ten seconds; the foghorn signal is one blast every 15 seconds.

The light was the last commissioned in the First U.S. Coast Guard District
and the only beacon in the region built by the maritime agency. It was
renovated by the U.S. Coast Guard in 1990 and is currently an active aid to
navigation. The beacon is not open to the public and is best viewed by boat.

Deer Island Light

Latitude: 42° 20' 24" N
Longitude: 70° 57' 18" W

Contact Information:
First U.S. Coast Guard District
408 Atlantic Avenue
Boston, Massachusetts 02210-3350
(617) 223-8243

Deer Island Light lies just south of Winthrop, Massachusetts, and 500 yards from the unsavory atoll from which it claims its name. Deer Island has long been a dumping ground, first as an internment camp for Native American captives during King Philip's War in the late 1600s, and then as the site for a prison and quarantine facility, where many immigrants died. Today it is the second largest wastewater treatment plant in the nation.

Deer Island Light

Winthrop, Massachusetts

Directions:
The light can be seen from Winthrop Beach, but the best views are from boat tours, including those operated by Boston Harbor Cruises, One Long Wharf, Boston, Massachusetts 02110; (617) 227-4321 or (877) 733-9425.

The first light at the site was a stone beacon built in 1832 with $3,000 from Congress. A proper lighthouse was erected at the site for $50,000 in 1890. It was a cast-iron "sparkplug" light painted chocolate brown with a fixed white light with a 2-second red flash every 30 seconds. The lighthouse sat on an iron caisson filled with concrete. Below its lantern room were five levels, including the crew's quarters.

During a devastating nor'easter in 1972, the lighthouse was abandoned. Damage from the storm was never repaired and the tower deteriorated throughout the 1970s. Deemed unsafe by the U.S. Coast Guard, the light was torn down and replaced in 1982 by an inelegant white fiberglass tower raised on the foundation of the old structure. The $100,000 spire was build in England and is believed to be the first fiberglass beacon in the country. When a storm destroyed the Great Point Light on Nantucket the following year, the U.S. Coast Guard planned to replace it with the fiberglass steeple from Deer Island. While the tower was removed from its Winthrop location, it was never used on Nantucket, as the residents there preferred a more esthetic wooden alternative.

Deer Island received a second fiberglass light, 51 feet tall and painted reddish brown, which remains an active aid to navigation.

Derby Wharf Light

Latitude: 42° 31' 00" N
Longitude: 70° 53' 00" W

Contact Information:
National Park Service
Salem National Historic Site
174 Derby Street
Salem, Massachusetts 01970
(978) 740-1660
Website: www.nps.gov/sama

Derby Wharf Light

Salem, Massachusetts

Directions:
Follow Route 1A into Salem. At the end of Route 1A, take a right onto Derby Street. Follow Derby Street to the Salem Maritime National Historic Site. The light will be at the end of the wharf. The light is closed to the public, but the grounds are open to visitors daily.

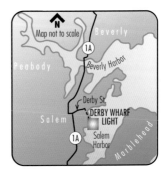

Salem's role as a international port of call was fading when the Derby Wharf light was lighted in 1871. The square brick lighthouse, originally equipped with a fifth-order Fresnel lens that shone a fixed red signal 25 feet above sea level, stands 23 feet high at the end of a dock that extends half a mile into Salem's inner harbor. For years, the twin lights on Bakers Island were considered sufficient for traffic into the trade center, but crowding in the inner harbor induced the community to build an additional light there for $3,000. With its close location to the city, a commuting caretaker operated the light rather than an on-site keeper.

In 1906, the beacon's optic was upgraded to a fourth-order Fresnel, but four years later, when the lighthouse was designated a harbor light, that optic was replaced with a sixth-order Fresnel, and its characteristic changed from a flashing to a fixed, red light. Electricity came to the station in the 1970s, when it became a flashing red light once again. The lighthouse was deactivated in 1977, and ownership was turned over to the National Park Service in 1979. Four years later, with the help of the Friends of Salem Maritime, the signal was revived as a private aid to navigation with a new 155-millimeter solar-powered optic. Today, the light is part of the Salem Maritime National Site, which was established in 1938.

Dog Bar Light and Eastern Point Light in distance

Latitude: 42° 34' 54" N
Longitude: 70° 40' 24" W

Contact Information:
First Coast Guard District
408 Atlantic Avenue
Boston, Massachusetts 02210-3350
(617) 223-8243

Dog Bar Light

Also known as Gloucester Breakwater
Gloucester, Massachusetts

Directions:
Follow Route 128 to the junction of Route 127A and East Main Street. Follow East Main Street until it becomes Eastern Point Road. Follow Eastern Point Road until it becomes Eastern Point Boulevard. Follow Eastern Point Boulevard. At the end of Eastern Point Boulevard is a parking lot. You can park there and access the breakwater on foot. The lighthouse is at the end of the breakwater. You can also view the lighthouse from harbor cruise ships leaving Gloucester, including those offered by Cape Ann Cruises (978-283-1979).

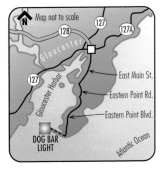

From 1894 to 1905, a 2,250-foot breakwater was constructed in Gloucester Harbor for $300,000. A 37-foot light was constructed at the end of the breakwater in 1905 to warn mariners of the dangerous Dog Bar Reef near the lighthouse.

The keeper of Eastern Point Light in Gloucester also had to tend the Dog Bar lighthouse, a treacherous task in winter when ice embraces the breakwater. Dual stewardship had certain benefits, too. During the fishing season, the breakwater is a Mecca for anglers, especially those looking to land bluefish.

The lighthouse—a small, white building elevated on a skeleton framework—went dark temporarily in 1931, when a gale washed away some of the breakwater's blocks and severed the power cable to the signal. Storms frequently rip boats from their moorings and have been known to toss a vessel over the 35-foot tall breakwater.

Automated in 1986 and currently an active aid to navigation, the beacon emits a fixed red light 45 feet above sea level. In foul weather, its foghorn sounds a single blast every 10 seconds.

Duxbury Pier (Bug Light)

Contact Information:
Project Gurnet & Bug Lights, Inc.
P.O. Box 2167
Duxbury, Massachusetts 02331
Website: www.buglight.org

Latitude: 41° 59' 12" N
Longitude: 70° 38' 54" W

The Duxbury Pier Lighthouse, raised in 1871 to warn mariners approaching Plymouth Bay of a dangerous shoal off Saquish Head, was the first offshore cast-iron caisson lighthouse built in the United States. The 47-foot conical tower, with integrated keeper's quarters, watchroom, and lantern room, rests on a cast-iron cylinder. The cylinder was towed to the site by barge, driven into the seabed, and crammed with concrete. Later, in 1886, the foundation was reinforced with 100 tons of riprap to further protect it from ships, ice floes, and the action of waves.

Because of their distinctive shape, caisson lighthouses were often given colorful names by nautical wags. The Duxbury light was first tagged

Duxbury Pier (Bug Light)

Duxbury, Massachusetts

Directions:
Duxbury Light can best be seen from the water. Plymouth Harbor Cruises (800-242-2449), located at Town Wharf, off Water Street, has cruises that offer scenic views of Duxbury Pier Light, Gurnet Point Light, the *Mayflower II*, and Plymouth Rock. To reach Plymouth Harbor Cruises from Boston, take Massachusetts Route 3 south (Southeast Expressway) to the Braintree split (Route 3), exit 7, Braintree/Cape Cod. Follow Route 3 to U.S. Route 44, exit 6A, Plymouth Center. Follow Route 44. When you cross Court Street, Route 44 becomes North Park Avenue. North Park Avenue feeds into a rotary. From the rotary, take Town Wharf Road to Town Wharf.

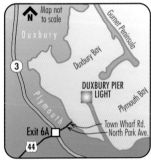

"The Coffee Pot." Later, after its outside decks were completed, it was called "Sparkplug," and because of its insect-like appearance from a distance, the "Bug Light."

When the light was automated in 1964, its original fourth-order Fresnel lens was removed and replaced with a modern optic. Without a human sentinel, the light suffered the slights of seabirds and vandals for 19 years. The damage was so severe that the U.S. Coast Guard planned to replace the signal with a fiberglass tower. Local residents and legislators, however, persuaded the Coast Guard to revise its plans, and the historic light was renovated in the 1980s. However, once the lease to the property held by the local group, called Project Bug Light, ran out, vandals descended on the lighthouse again. They defiled the lantern room, leaving the interior exposed to the weather. As the elements took their toll on the defaced structure, the U.S. Coast Guard revived its plans for a fiberglass replacement. Nevertheless, Project Bug Light was revived and the light rejuvenated in 1996. In 1999, the Coast Guard leased Plymouth Light to the local group, which changed its name to Project Gurnet & Bug Lights to reflect its new responsibilities.

East Chop Light

Latitude: 41° 28' 12" N
Longitude: 70° 34' 06" W

Contact Information:
Martha's Vineyard Historical Society
P.O. Box 1310
59 School Street (Pease House)
Edgartown, Massachusetts 02539
(508) 627-4441
Fax: (508) 627-4436

East Chop Light

Oak Bluffs (Martha's Vineyard), Massachusetts

Directions:
From the Vineyard Haven ferry, turn left onto Beach Road. Follow to Eastville Avenue. Turn left onto Temahegin Avenue. Follow to Highland Drive. Turn left onto Highland Drive. Follow to lighthouse. Sunset tours are offered by the historical society on Sundays from mid-June to mid-September. Tours are available from an hour and a half before sunset to half an hour after. Admission for an adult is $3.

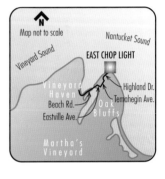

Originally the site of a semaphore station, East Chop received its first lighthouse in 1869, thanks to Silas Daggett, a civic-minded captain who felt a beacon was needed on the headland known as Telegraph Hill to guide ships entering Vineyard Haven Harbor. Supported by the kindness of local merchants, Daggett operated his lighthouse privately. Fire destroyed the signal in 1871, but the plucky seaman rebuilt it as a light atop his home. Later, Daggett sold the site to the government for $5,000, and in 1878, a new light adorned East Chop. Made of cast iron with a concrete foundation, the conical beacon was 40 feet high with a 79-foot focal plane. Until 1988, the tower, now white, was painted an odd reddish-brown, which earned it the nickname "The Chocolate Lighthouse."

The original fourth-order Fresnel lens was replaced with an acrylic lens in 1984. The 300-millimeter optic flashes green for three seconds followed by darkness for three seconds and is visible for 15 miles.

After the light was automated in 1933, the Coast Guard offered to rent the keeper's house for $100 a month to its current inhabitant, George Walter Purdy, a former lobsterman who lost an arm in an engine room accident aboard the lighthouse tender *Azalea*. Purdy rebuffed the offer, and the Coast Guard demolished the dwelling along with an oil building at the site.

Eastern Point Light

Latitude: 42° 34' 48" N
Longitude: 70° 39' 54" W

Contact Information:
First U.S. Coast Guard District
408 Atlantic Avenue
Boston, Massachusetts 02210-3350
(617) 223-8243

Eastern Point Light

Gloucester, Massachusetts

Directions:
From the junction of Routes 127A and 128 in Gloucester, follow East Main Street until it becomes Eastern Point Road. Follow Eastern Point Road until it turns into Eastern Point Boulevard and follow to its end. There's a parking area there. "Private Road" signs are posted on the road to the light, but access to the lighthouse is allowed.

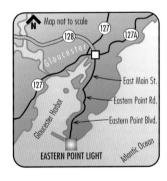

Once the home of renowned American artist Winslow Homer, Eastern Point in Gloucester has hosted beacons for mariners since 1832. One of the Point's distinguished landmarks is Beauport, a 40-room mansion, now a museum, where such visitors as Henry James, Noel Coward, and Eleanor Roosevelt were once wined and dined.

The initial lighthouse, situated at the end of the rocky peninsula on the eastern side of Gloucester Harbor, was first lighted in 1832. Built for $2,450, it was a 30-foot stone tower that emitted a fixed white light. Not an engineering miracle, a good blow often shook the light's lantern so hard its glass would fissure.

A new beacon supplanted the old one in 1848. The 34-foot fanal became known as the Ruby Light because the French red plate glass surrounding its lantern gave the signal a fixed red characteristic. The light's range was boosted from 11 to 13 miles in 1857 when its 11 whale oil lamps were swapped for a fourth-order Fresnel lens.

The current light was constructed in 1890. The conical white tower is 36 feet tall and made of brick with a stone foundation. A two-story Gothic Revival wooden keeper's house erected in 1879 is also at the site. The lighthouse's original optic, now on display at the Cape Ann Historical Association Museum in Gloucester, was replaced in 1994 with a DCB-24. Automated in 1985, the light, which flashes white every 5 seconds 57 feet above sea level, remains an active aid to navigation.

Edgartown Harbor Light

Latitude: 41° 23' 27" N
Longitude: 70° 30' 11" W

Contact Information:
Martha's Vineyard Historical Society
P.O. Box 1310
59 School Street (Pease House)
Edgartown, Massachusetts 02539
(508) 627-4441 Fax: (508) 627-4436

The current Edgartown Harbor Light was barged to its present location from Crane's Beach in Ipswich, Massachusetts, in 1939. The 1938 "Long Island Express," a hurricane in New England that caused $20 billion in damage and took 600 lives, mortally damaged the original herald to the

Edgartown Harbor Light

Edgartown (Martha's Vineyard), Massachusetts

Directions:
From Main Street in the center of Edgartown take North Water Street to Starbuck Neck Road. The lighthouse is located on Lighthouse Beach at Starbuck's Neck just beyond the end of Starbuck Neck Road. Street parking is frequently difficult because of congestion. The lighthouse is a little over a half-mile walk from the intersection of Main and North Water. A shuttle bus is also available to the site.

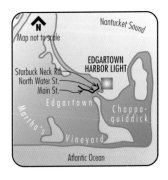

harbor's entrance. That herald was an 1828 two-story Cape house with a lantern room on its roof built for $5,500. It sat on a small, artificial island 1,300 feet from shore. In 1830, a wooden pier to the island was built for $2,500. It became known as the "Bridge of Sighs" because whalemen met their wives and lovers there before departing for sea. Fire destroyed the pier several times, and it was replaced with a stone breakwater in 1847 for $4,700.

When the U.S. Coast Guard tried to replace the damaged light with a steel beacon tower, the move was quashed by local opposition intent on preserving their town's architectural esthetic. Hence the current tower, built in 1875, was floated to Edgartown from Boston's North Shore. Made of cast iron on a foundation of granite blocks, the 45-foot conical light has a focal plane of 45 feet. The tower's original automated lens was replaced in 1988 with a solar-powered 250-millimeter optic. That optic flashes red every 6 seconds over a range of 5 nautical miles.

Over the years, sand filled the area between the light and the mainland. Today, the beacon, which briefly appeared in the 1975 movie *Jaws*, sits on its own beach. Surrounding the tower are 2,000 cobblestones reserved for the names of deceased children. They are part of a memorial established in 2001 by the current leasee of the property, the Martha's Vineyard Historical Society.

Fort Pickering (Winter Island) Light

Latitude: 42° 31' 36" N
Longitude: 70° 52' 00" W

Contact Information:
Winter Island: A Marine Recreational Park
Charlie Arnold, Manager
50 Winter Island Road
Salem, Massachusetts 01970
(978) 745-9430 Fax: (978) 745-1875
E-mail: winterisland@cove.com
Website: www.salemweb.com/winterisland

Fort Pickering Light is located on an engaging piece of real estate in Salem harbor called Winter Island. A fort has been on the island, which is connected to the city by a bridge of land, since the 1600s. In 1944, the first U.S. Coast Guard air-sea rescue station on the East Coast was located there.

Fort Pickering (Winter Island) Light

Salem, Massachusetts

Directions:
Take Route 1A into Salem and take a right onto Derby Street, which will become Fort Avenue. Follow Fort Avenue to Winter Island Road and turn right. At the end of the road is the entrance to Winter Island Park. After entering the park, stay to the left, and the road will lead you to the lighthouse.

The lighthouse was built in 1871. Together with Derby Wharf Light, also lighted in that year, the duo gave mariners a firm fix of their position in the harbor.

Shining a flashing white light 28 feet above sea level, the 32-foot Fort Pickering Light is a cast-iron cylinder reinforced from within with brick. Originally painted red, the light is now white.

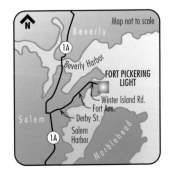

When the U.S. Coast Guard deserted the island in 1969, the lighthouse suffered from neglect. In the legendary blizzard of 1978, the lighthouse's door was ripped from the structure and sent to the deep. In the 1980s, concerned citizens formed the Fort Pickering Light Association and began restoring the light, starting by reclaiming the light's door from beneath the foamy brine. In 1983, the beacon shone once again as a private aid to navigation, but in 1995, it went black when the conduit for its power lines deteriorated. Later that year, a new solar-powered, 300-millimeter optic was installed for $2,300, a cost split by the city and association.

In 1999, the beacon received a substantial makeover. Some $13,800 in iron work, painting, and glass restoration financed with public money was performed by the American Steeple Corporation, a local company whose résumé includes refurbishment of the tower of the Old North Church in Boston and the Church of the Presidents in Quincy.

Gay Head Light

Latitude: 41° 20' 54" N
Longitude: 70° 50' 06" W

Contact Information:
Martha's Vineyard Historical Society
P.O. Box 1310
59 School Street (Pease House)
Edgartown, Massachusetts 02539
(508) 627-4441
Fax: (508) 627-4436

Distinctive with its redbrick and sandstone facade, the light at Gay Head on the western side of Martha's Vineyard stands at a site with navigational credentials dating back to 1799. The first lighthouse atop Gay Head's 130-foot multicolored clay cliffs was an octagonal tower costing $5,750. Built when there were only 15 lighthouses on the East Coast of the United States, the lighthouse warned mariners of the treacherous Devil's Bridge ledge, the scene of one of New England's worst maritime disasters: the sinking in 1884 of the S.S. *City of Columbus*, in which 100 passengers drowned in 20 minutes.

The current 51-foot conical tower, which has a focal plane of 170 feet, was built in 1856. It was equipped with an enormous first-order Fresnel lens with 1,008 prisms, imported from France, where it had been exhibited at the

Gay Head Light

Aquinnah (Martha's Vineyard), Massachusetts

Directions:
Take the ferry to Martha's Vineyard from Woods Hole, Falmouth, Hyannis, New Bedford, New London (Connecticut), or Montauk (New York). From Vineyard Haven landing, take a right on Beach Road and travel west 1.8 miles to State Road. Turn left onto State Road. Take State Road 2.6 miles to North Road and turn right. Follow 5.7 miles to Menemsha Cross Road and turn left. Follow 1 mile to State Road. Turn right onto State Road.

Follow 3 miles to lighthouse. The historical society offers sunset tours on Friday, Saturday, and Sunday from mid-June to mid-September. Tours are available from an hour and a half before sunset to half an hour after. Admission is $3 for adults, and children under 12 are free. The tower is open free to the public on Mother's Day.

Paris World Fair. Replaced in 1953 with a DCB-224 Aerobeacon, the original Fresnel can be seen at the Martha's Vineyard Historical Society. The Aero lens, which flashes alternately red and white every 15 seconds, was initially developed by Carlisle & Finch Company of Cincinnati, Ohio, for airport applications, but the model became a popular fixture in 1950s lighthouses.

In 1902, the keeper's brick abode was razed—a response to fatal illnesses contracted by several of the light's inhabitants and attributed to the dampness of their living quarters—and replaced with a wooden house on a higher foundation. That house was demolished in 1956, and the light became fully automated in 1960.

The Graves Light

Latitude: 42° 21' 54" N
Longitude: 70° 52' 06" W

Contact Information:
The Friends of the Boston Harbor Islands
P.O. Box 690187
Quincy, Massachusetts 02269-0187
(781) 740-4290
E-mail: fbhi@earthlink.net   Website: www.fbhi.org

While the necessity for a lighthouse at the ledges known as The Graves—named for Thomas Graves, appointed a vice admiral of the navy by the Bay State's first governor, John Winthrop—was identified as early as 1842, it was not until the turn of the century and the opening of the Broad Sound Channel at the northern entrance to Boston Harbor that construction began.

Built between 1903 and 1905, the 113-foot conical granite tower is a marvel of lighthouse engineering. Stone for the structure was quarried at Rockport, Massachusetts, carted to Lovell's Island, and ferried by schooner

The Graves Light

Winthrop, Massachusetts

Directions:
The Graves Light is not open to the public and is best viewed by boat, but it can be seen at a distance from Little Brewster Island, the location of Boston Light; Shore Drive in Winthrop; Nantasket Beach in Hull; and Nahant. Excursion cruises that offer views of the beacon are offered by the Friends of Boston Harbor Islands and Boston Harbor Cruises, One Long Wharf, Boston, Massachusetts 02110; (617) 227-4321 or (877) 733-9425.

3.5 miles to the work site. A shanty for some 30 workers was erected on the highest ledge at the site. It was connected to a wharf by a 90-foot elevated walkway and contained living quarters, a storeroom, a blacksmith shop, and a kitchen.

The lighthouse was equipped with the most potent light in Massachusetts history: a first-order Fresnel lens that was 9 feet in diameter, stood 12 feet high, and sat on 400 pounds of mercury. Its brightness rated at 380,000 candlepower, which was later upgraded to 3.2 million candlepower.

Long a salty grave for many a ship, the most famous wreck at the site was the *City of Salisbury*, also known as the Zoo Ship, which sank in 1938 with $1 million in cargo aboard. No human life was lost in the mishap, and most of the ship's consignment of exotic animals was removed from the vessel before it split in two on an uncharted pinnacle of rock off Graves Ledge.

In 1976, the light was automated and its Fresnel lens shipped to the Smithsonian. Its new lens, a DCB-224, was powered from an underwater cable originating in Hull, Massachusetts. This problematic arrangement was eliminated in 2001 when the lighthouse, still an active aid to navigation today, was outfitted with solar-powered VRB-25 optic.

Great Point Light

Contact Information:
Coskata-Coatue Wildlife Refuge
Wauwinet Road
Wauwinet, Nantucket, Massachusetts
(508) 228-5646
E-mail: islands@ttor.org

Latitude: 41° 23' 24" N
Longitude: 70° 02' 54" W

In 1770, Nantucket petitioned the state for a lighthouse to guide ships cruising the waters between Great Point and Monomoy Island, just south of Chatham, Massachusetts. The matter was tabled for 14 years, but eventually a wooden beacon was raised at the site.

As wooden buildings consuming large quantities of flammable liquids are prone to do, the lighthouse turned into flare in 1816. A new light replaced it in 1818—a 60-foot stone tower constructed for $7,500.

Great Point Light

Nantucket, Massachusetts

Directions:
From Nantucket center, follow Orange Street south to the rotary. From the rotary, take Milestone Road east to Polpis Road. Follow Polpis Road for 6 miles. Turn left onto Wauwinet Road and drive to the end to the gatehouse. The lighthouse is 7 miles across The Galls from Wauwinet. The Trustees of Reservations offers daily three-hour tours of the lighthouse by over-sand vehicle from June through October at 9:30 A.M. and 1:30 P.M. Tour groups are limited to eight persons, including children. Reservations are required and can be obtained by calling (508) 228-6799. The light is also accessible by 4-wheel-drive vehicle with an over-sand permit.

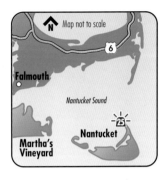

In 1857, that signal received a third-order Fresnel lens.

From 1863 to 1890, a lightship in the sound competed with the beacon for the mariners' attention, creating a virtual demolition derby on the water. During the period, there were 43 shipwrecks, five of them involving collisions with the lightship. Finally, in 1889, the problem was remedied by giving Great Point a fixed red sector to distinguish it from the lightship.

Great Point Light was automated in the 1950s. The keeper's house was destroyed by fire in 1966. Despite pleas from locals to move the light farther inland to avoid the effects of erosion, the U.S. Coast Guard failed to act. Eventually, the sea severely compromised the beacon's foundation, and in 1984 a nor'easter reduced it to rubble.

The current light was built 300 yards from its predecessor's location for $1.14 million. The white, conical concrete tower is 60 feet tall with a focal plane of 71 feet. It has a solar-powered optic, which flashes white every 5 seconds and has a red sector from 84 to 106 degrees.

Highland (Cape Cod) Light

Contact Information:
Cape Cod National Seashore
(508) 255-3421
Website: www.nps.gov

Latitude: 42° 02' 18" N
Longitude: 70° 03' 42" W

Precariously perched on a 125-foot bluff in Truro, Massachusetts, Highland Light, also known as Cape Cod Light, was the first lighthouse built on Cape Cod. Erected in 1797 to warn seafarers of the treacherous Peaked Hill Bars 3 miles northeast of the signal, the original 45-foot-high wooden structure pierced the night with a beam shining 160 feet above sea level and illuminated by 24 lamps burning sperm whale oil.

Erosion soon menaced the wooden tower, and it was supplanted with a new brick beacon around 1831. That lighthouse, too, was victimized by the gnawing elements. In 1857, it was replaced by a 66-foot brick tower

Highland (Cape Cod) Light

Truro, Massachusetts

Directions:
From Boston, take Massachusetts Route 3 (Southeast Expressway) to U.S. Route 6. Follow Route 6 to South Hollow Road in North Truro. Turn right onto South Hollow Road. Follow to South Highland Road. Turn left onto South Highland Road, then turn right onto Highland Light Road. There is a parking area with a path to the lighthouse. The grounds of the lighthouse are open daily year-round. From May 1 to October, the light's tower is open for guided tours. A small fee is charged to climb the tower. The Highland Museum and its souvenir shop are located in the keeper's house.

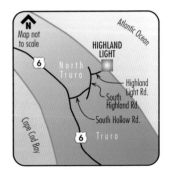

equipped with a powerful first-order Fresnel lens and a Queen Anne-style keeper's house attached. When the lighthouse's illumination characteristics were changed to flashing white from fixed white in 1901, its lens was upgraded. The new Fresnel floated on a bed of mercury to achieve the flashing effect.

At the turn of the century, early experiments in wireless communication were conducted at the site. A U.S. Navy wireless telegraph station to communicate with ships at sea was set up in 1904. Radio beacons were also tested at the site. These allow a vessel's position to be fixed during foul weather.

In 1932, the signal was electrified and outfitted with a new 1,000-watt lamp rated at four million candlepower and visible for 39 nautical miles. The Fresnel was replaced in the 1950s with twin rotating aerobeacons. That optic was replaced with a VRB-25 Aerobeacon in 1998.

During the 1990s, the encroaching Atlantic once again imperiled the light (which was automated in 1986), and in 1996, $1.5 million was raised to move the 450-ton structure on steel tracks lubricated with Ivory soap 570 feet inland, where its beam shines 183 feet above sea level.

Hospital Point Front Range Light

Latitude: 42° 32' 48" N
Longitude: 70° 51' 24" W

Hospital Point Rear Range Light

Latitude: 42° 32' 53" N
Longitude: 70° 52' 42" W

Contact Information:
First Coast Guard District
408 Atlantic Avenue
Boston, Massachusetts 02210-3350
(617) 223-8243

Hospital Point had a rich history before the addition of a lighthouse to the area in 1872. It garnered its name from a smallpox hospital erected there in 1801. Used as a military barracks during the War of 1812, the hospital was destroyed in a conflagration in 1849.

Hospital Point Front and Rear Range Lights

Beverly, Massachusetts

Directions:
Although closed to the public, the U.S. Coast Guard opens the lighthouse for tours in August during Beverly Homecoming Week. The station is best seen by boat, but can be viewed distantly from Salem Willows Park in Salem, or more closely from Bayview Avenue in Beverly. To get to Bayview Avenue from Boston, take Route 93 north to U.S. Route 95/128. Follow Route 95 north until it splits with Route 128. Follow Route 128 to exit 18. At the end of the exit ramp, follow Old Essex Road to Route 22. Take Route 22 south to Corning Street. Follow Corning Street, which becomes East Corning Street, to Bayview Avenue. Follow Bayview Avenue to the light.

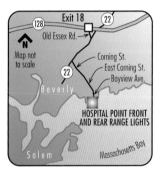

The Federal-style keeper's house and 45-foot light tower are quite distinctive. The square white lighthouse built of brick with a granite foundation sports a 3.5-order Fresnel lens and emits a fixed white signal 70 feet above sea level. Shielding the lens is a unique condensing panel that from the sea reduces the intensity of the light should a mariner stray from the main channel into Salem harbor.

When a second signal made from the remains of a lightship was built in the steeple of Beverly's First Baptist Church a mile away in 1927, the light was officially dubbed the Hospital Point Rear Range Light. The steeple was the only portion of the church to survive a devastating blaze in 1975.

Hospital Point Light was automated in 1947. At that time, the station became the permanent home of the commanders of the First U.S. Coast Guard District. Both the steeple beacon and Hospital Point Light are active aids to navigation.

Hyannis Harbor Light

Latitude: 41° 38' 56" N
Longitude: 70° 16' 34" W

Contact Information:
Privately owned

While Nantucket prospered from the oil of leviathans, so did its neighbor, Hyannis. The town became the island's primary link to the mainland as well as a busy commercial port.

As sea traffic grew, so did the demand for a lighthouse to mark the treacherous waters southwest of the harbor. Congress met that demand in 1848 and appropriated $2,000 for a beacon. The construction of a 20-foot, white conical tower with a black lantern room was finished in 1849. Shining 43 feet above sea level for a distance of 8 miles, the brick dwelling had a fixed white signal with a red sector to warn off shellbacks from Eddie Woods Rock, Southwest Rock, and Southwest Ground Shoal.

Hyannis Harbor Light

Hyannis, Massachusetts

Directions:
From Boston, take Route 3 south (Southeast Expressway) to Route 6 over the Sagamore Bridge to exit 6, Route 132, into Hyannis. At the airport rotary, take the second right onto Barnstable Road, which becomes Ocean Street (after the intersection at Old Colony Road and South Street). Follow to Gosnold Street. Turn right onto Gosnold Street. Follow to Harbor Road. Turn left onto Harbor Road and drive to the end. The lighthouse will be on the right, but it is private property.

Originally fitted with three oil lamps with reflectors, the light received a sixth-order Fresnel lens in 1856, two years after a railhead was established in the town for the Cape Cod Railroad, which was merged with the Old Colony Railroad in 1872.

The lighthouse became a rear range light in 1885 when a front range light was raised on the Old Colony Railroad wharf. At the turn of the 20th century, a shipping lane was dredged open to Hyannis's inner harbor. With traffic diverted to that harbor, Hyannis Light lost its usefulness. In 1929, the tower's lantern room, renovated in 1863, was removed and its functions replaced by Hyannis Harbor Breakwater Light. The keeper's house and tower were sold at auction to private interests. A new lantern room, without an optic, was added to the tower in 1987.

Isles of Shoals Light

Latitude: 42° 58' 00" N
Longitude: 70° 37' 24" W

Contact Information:
New Hampshire Division of Parks and Recreation
P.O. Box 1856
Concord, NH 03302-1856
(603) 271-3556
E-mail: nhparks@dred.state.nh.us

Isles of Shoals Light

Also known as White Island Light
White Island, New Hampshire

Directions:
Isles of Shoals Light, New Hampshire's only off-shore lighthouse, is located on White Island, a private island 10 miles off the coast of Portsmouth, New Hampshire. The lighthouse can be viewed by boat only. There are several lighthouse cruises that tour the area, including Isles of Shoals Steamship Company, (800) 441-4620 and Portsmouth Harbor Cruises, (800) 776-0915.

The first Isles of Shoals Light was constructed on White Island, off the coast of Portsmouth, New Hampshire, in 1820. It was built as a stone tower and later encased by wood and shingled. Although a new lantern and lighting apparatus were installed in 1841, a Fresnel lens was not put in place until 1855. The current white-brick-over-granite, 58-foot-tall lighthouse tower was built in 1859 and outfitted with a second-order Fresnel lens. The tower, with a focal point of 82 feet, was built with 2-foot-thick walls because of the dangers from Civil War blockade runners and Southern gunboats.

The light was automated in 1987 and today is a VRB-25 solar-powered optic. It flashes white every 15 seconds and can be seen for 15 miles. The fog signal sounds one blast every 30 seconds. Today, Isles of Shoals Light is the property of the State of New Hampshire, which reclaimed it from the Coast Guard in 1993 (although the light is still maintained by the Coast Guard as an active aid to navigation). It is managed by the New Hampshire Division of Parks and Recreation. In recent years the lighthouse tower had fallen into disrepair, with significant cracks in its brick exterior. Thanks in part to the efforts of a group of New Hampshire schoolchildren calling themselves The Lighthouse Kids, in 2003 the lighthouse received a $250,000 Save America's Treasures grant and restorations are underway.

Long Island Light

Latitude: 42° 19' 48" N
Longitude: 70° 57' 30" W

Contact Information:
First U.S. Coast Guard District
408 Atlantic Avenue
Boston, Massachusetts 02210-3350
(617) 223-8243

Besides being the purported location of the nation's first cast-iron lighthouse, Long Island in Boston Harbor has been home to a resort hotel, a hospital, military fortifications, and a legendary ghost.

The apparition is said to be the spirit of Mary Burton, a British trooper's wife killed during the Revolutionary War. In 1776, Burton and her spouse were aboard a vessel in Boston Harbor. American forces engaged the ship, and in the ensuing melee, Mary died from a head wound caused by a can-

Directions:
Although Long Island was connected to the mainland by a bridge from Quincy in 1951, the public is not allowed to reach the island by land. Thus, the light is best seen from the water. Several excursion boats pass by the signal, including those operated by Boston Harbor Cruises, One Long Wharf, Boston, Massachusetts 02110; (617) 227-4321 or (877) 733-9425.

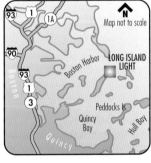

nonball. Her husband buried her in a red blanket on Long Island. Soon reports began appearing about a woman's anguished nocturnal cries heard in the vicinity of Long Head. Later, a "lady in Scarlet," blood pouring from her pate, was seen haunting the area.

If Burton did haunt Long Head, her ghost didn't deter builders from erecting a 23-foot, granite-and-rubblestone beacon at the site in 1819. Over the years, that light deteriorated, and it was replaced in 1844. The 21-foot edifice, prefabricated by the South Boston Iron Company, was tapered—its diameter is 12 feet at the base and 6 feet at the top.

Cast iron proved to be a durable material, and the light did not have to be replaced again until 1881, when another ferrous fanal was raised at the site, as well as a new keeper's house. That light lasted a scant 10 years. At the turn of the century, a military installation on the island was enlarged and the iron signal supplanted with a 52-foot brick lighthouse at a new location on the key. The new lighthouse was equipped with a fourth-order Fresnel lens that displayed a fixed, white light 120 feet above sea level.

The beacon was automated in 1918 and deactivated in 1982; it was renovated and its new solar-powered optic relighted in 1985. Today it remains an active aid to navigation.

Long Point Light

Contact Information:
American Lighthouse Foundation
P.O. Box 889
Wells, Maine 04090
(207) 646-0245
E-mail: alf@lighthousefoundation.org

Latitude: 42° 01' 59" N
Longitude: 70° 10' 07" W

Since the early 1800s, a lighthouse at Long Point has illumined the entrance to the harbor at Provincetown, once home to the largest whaling fleet outside Nantucket and New Bedford and still the base for the largest commercial fishing fleet on Cape Cod.

The first light at the point, raised in 1826 for $16,000, was a tower and lantern room protruding from the roof of a wooden keeper's house. It emitted a fixed white light visible for 13 nautical miles.

Long Point Light

Provincetown, Massachusetts

Directions:
Take U.S. Route 6 to Provincetown. The light can be seen from Pilgrim's Monument or Macmillan's Wharf. To walk to the light, go to the end of Commercial Street to the Pilgrim's Landing area. From there, a breakwater can be accessed. Follow the breakwater. It's about a half mile long. The walk from the end of the breakwater to the light is about an hour over sand. The trip should be planned at low tide because portions of the breakwater are under water at high tide. A round-trip journey takes approximately 4 hours. A water shuttle to the light is offered by Flyer's, 131A Commercial Street, (508) 487-0898 (flyersrentals.com).

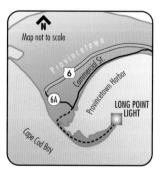

The lighthouse's original Lewis patent lamps were replaced with a sixth-order Fresnel lens in 1856, just before two Civil War redoubts were built at the point in 1861. The fortifications were built in anticipation of a rebel blockade of the harbor. As the war progressed and that notion became more and more dubious, the fortresses became known as Fort Useless and Fort Ridiculous.

After an inspector cautioned that the light could be severely jeopardized in heavy weather, $13,000 was appropriated by Congress for a new lighthouse. In 1875, a 38-foot, square, brown tower made of brick, a one-and-half-story keeper's house, and a 1,200-pound fog bell were erected at the site. The beacon, which was later painted white, shone a fixed white light through a fifth-order Fresnel lens. An oil building was added to the complex in 1904.

The Fresnel was upgraded to a more modern optic and the signal automated in 1952. In 1982, the facility's optic was replaced again with a 300-millimeter optic powered by solar panels. The light remains an active aid to navigation.

Marblehead Light

Contact Information:
Marblehead Chamber of Commerce
P.O. Box 76
62 Pleasant Street
Marblehead, Massachusetts 01945
(781) 631-2868

Latitude: 42° 30' 18" N
Longitude: 70° 50' 00" W

Although Marblehead is one of the most picturesque communities in Massachusetts, the lighthouse that bears the town's name is far from pleasing to viewers. The 105-foot beacon built in 1896 looks like a lantern impaled on a brown stovepipe cocooned with iron bracing.

That was not always the case. The original light was quaint. Erected at Marblehead Neck in 1835 for $4,500, it was a 20-foot conical white tower with a beacon that could be seen for 12 miles. A covered walkway connected the lighthouse to the Victorian keeper's house, whose gables were charmingly embellished with gingerbread woodwork.

Marblehead Light

Marblehead, Massachusetts

Directions:
From Boston, take Massachusetts Route 1A north to Atlantic Avenue (Route 129) in Swampscott. Follow Atlantic Avenue north to Beach Street in Marblehead. Take a right onto Beach Street. Follow to the intersection with Ocean Avenue. Bear right on Ocean Avenue. Follow to Harbor Avenue. Bear left onto Harbor Avenue. Follow until it reconnects with Ocean Avenue. Follow Ocean Avenue to Chandler Hovey Park. The lighthouse is not open to the public, but it can be approached from the park.

As Marblehead's reputation as a summer resort grew, the lighthouse was soon dwarfed by "cottages" built by affluent seasonal residents, and it could no longer be seen by ships at sea. A makeshift solution was deployed in 1883, when a lantern atop a 100-foot mast was raised at the site, but by 1896 it was decided that a more steadfast alternative was needed, and the current signal was constructed.

The tower was originally equipped with a sixth-order Fresnel lens and kerosene lamp that emitted a fixed white light, later changed to fixed red. Today, the light shines fixed green 130 feet above sea level. In 1956, the Marblehead selectpeople attempted to improve the esthetics of the light by requesting that the U.S. Coast Guard paint the structure white. Their request was denied.

The original keeper's house was removed from the site in 1959. The following year the light was automated, and its Fresnel was swapped for a 300-millimeter modern optic. Still an active aid to navigation, the light is surrounded by a park fashioned from land given to Marblehead in 1948 by local resident and yachtsman Chandler Hovey.

Minot's Ledge Light

Latitude: 42° 16' 12" N
Longitude: 70° 45' 30" W

Contact Information:
Cohasset Chamber of Commerce
P.O. Box 336
Cohasset, MA 02025
(781) 383-1010
Website: www.cohassetchamber.org/index.htm

Despite the reputation of Minot's Ledge as one of the most perilous obstructions to navigation on the East Coast, it was not until 1847 that construction began on the first light at the site.

Minot's Ledge Light

Cohasset, Massachusetts

Directions:
Minot's Ledge is best viewed by boat, but the light can be seen from a distance at Sandy Beach in Cohasset. To get to Sandy Beach, take Route 3A (King Street) and take a left onto Sohler Street. Turn right on North Main Street and follow it to Beach Street. Take a left off Beach Street at Atlantic Avenue and proceed to the beach parking lot.

From 1832 to 1841 alone, the ledge sent more than 40 vessels to Davey Jones' Locker. But building a lighthouse at that location, which was exposed to the full fury of the Atlantic, was no easy task. Initially, lighthouse builders jilted traditional designs in favor of a 70-foot, cast-iron "spider" that took three years to erect at a cost of $39,000.

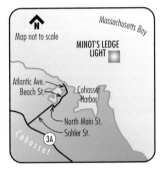

Sixteen months into service, admonitions about the spider light's instability were fulfilled when a catastrophic storm washed away the beacon and the lives of two assistant keepers.

The construction of a new lighthouse proved to be a formidable task, and for the next 9 years, ships had to be warned off the ledge by a lightship. Work began on a replacement tower in 1855, but labor on the project could be done only at low tide and during fair weather. Even in opportune conditions, laborers were often swept into the sea by crashing waves.

What has been called one of the greatest achievements of American lighthouse engineering was completed in 1860 at a cost of $330,000, one of the most expensive navigational aids in U.S. history. Originally equipped with a second-order Fresnel lens with 110,000 candlepower, the 97-foot conical tower has endured much, including being hit by a 176-foot wave. The light was fully automated in 1947. Today it has a solar-powered optic rated at 45,000 candlepower that can be seen from 15 miles away.

Monomoy Point Light

Latitude: 41° 33' 33" N
Longitude: 69° 59' 37" W

Contact Information:
Cape Cod Museum of Natural History
869 Route 6A
Brewster, Massachusetts 02631
(508) 896-3867 Fax: (508) 896-8844
E-mail: info@ccmnh.org

It has been bombed and machine-gunned, but Monomoy Point Light still stands.

The waters around Monomoy are some of the most dangerous in the Northeast. It is said that the shallow shoals and strong rip currents there induced the Pilgrims to settle in Massachusetts Bay and not extend their voyage to Virginia.

Monomoy Point Light

Chatham, Massachusetts

Directions:
The lighthouse is accessible only by boat. The Audubon Society of Wellfleet and the Cape Cod Museum of Natural History in Brewster both offer trips to the light. Monomoy Island is accessible by private boat. After coming ashore on the island, you can hike to the light.

Raised in 1823, the first beacon at Monomoy Island, which is 9 miles south of Chatham, Massachusetts, was a wooden tower with an iron lantern room on the roof of a brick, Cape Cod-style keeper's house. Together with Great Point Light on Nantucket, the light marked the entrance to Nantucket Sound.

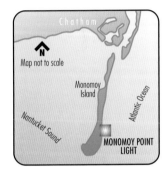

Battling wind, surf, and storm took its toll on the lighthouse, and in 1849 a new 40-foot tower with a black lantern room was constructed, as well as a two-story Cape Cod-style keeper's house. Although conical construction was stronger and masonry structures more durable, a cast-iron cylinder was used for the signal. That decision later required that the beacon be reinforced with a brick lining to improve its stability and strength.

In 1855, the tower was equipped with a fourth-order Fresnel lens, which shone 47 feet above sea level for 12 miles. In 1882, the tower was painted red to improve its visibility, and in 1892, the light's stability was enhanced with iron trusses.

With the opening of Cape Cod Canal in 1914, sea traffic was diverted from Nantucket Sound and the Monomoy lighthouse's usefulness waned. It was decommissioned in 1923 and its lens removed. Although the U.S. Navy used the property for bombing and machine-gun practice during World War II, the buildings, remarkably, averted serious damage. In 1944, the area became a wildlife refuge, and in 1989, the site was totally renovated.

Nantucket Lightship

Latitude: N/A
Longitude: N/A

Contact Information:
The Nantucket Lightship WLV-612
P.O. Box 3185
Waquot, MA 02536
(617) 821-6771
E-mail: info@nantucketlightship.com
Website: www.nantucketlightship.com

Nantucket Lightship

Rowes Wharf, Nantucket Island, Massachusetts

Directions to Rowes Wharf:

From north: Take Route 93 south to the High Street/Congress Street exit. Follow ramp and take left onto Congress Street. Follow to Atlantic Avenue and turn left. Rowes Wharf is two blocks down on the right.

From south: Take Route 93 north to the South Station/Mass Pike exit. Follow signs to Atlantic Avenue and South Station. Rowes Wharf is about .5 mile on the right.

Lightship 612 was constructed in Curtis Bay, Maryland, in 1950 and served as the *San Francisco* for 18 years and the *Blunts Reef* for two years before returning to the East Coast. After a four-year stint in Maine as the *Portland*, the 612 was stationed in Massachusetts in 1975 as the *Nantucket*. The steel 128-foot vessel, the last manned lightship in the United States, was decommissioned on March 29, 1985. She was purchased by the Boston Marine Exchange, but a lack of funding caused the group to abandon its plans and the ship was acquired by the Commonwealth of Massachusetts and docked at Quincy's Marina Bay, where it was cared for by a partnership of state government and the nonprofit Friends of the Nantucket Lightship.

In 2000, Massachusetts decided to sell the ship and auctioned her on the Internet auction site Ebay. Fortunately, at $126,100, former state senator Bill Golden and his wife, Kristen, were the high bidders and saved the nearly fifty-year-old ship from being sold for scrap metal. After a four-year refit and restoration by the Goldens, the *Nantucket* now serves as a luxurious private yacht available for charter in either Nantucket Harbor (May through September) or at Rowes Wharf, Boston (October through April).

Nauset Light

Latitude: 41° 51' 36" N
Longitude: 69° 57' 12" W

Contact Information:
The Nauset Light Preservation Society
P.O. Box 941, Eastham, Massachusetts 02642
(508) 240-2612
E-mail: ssabin@capecod.net

When the 90-ton, cast-iron tower now known as Nauset Light arrived at its new craggy home in 1923, erosion from the fierce Atlantic waters had pulled to her bosom a trio of lights first built at the location in 1838, forcing two to pull up stakes in 1911, and threatening the third.

Nauset Light

Eastham, Massachusetts

Directions:

Take Massachusetts Route 3 south (Southeast Expressway) to Route 6 over the Sagamore Bridge. Continue on Route 6 to Eastham. At the third traffic signal from the Eastham/ Orleans rotary, turn right onto Bracket Road. Drive to the end of Bracket Road and turn left onto Nauset Road. Follow Nauset Road to Cable Road. Turn right onto Cable Road. At the end of Cable Road, turn left onto Ocean View Drive and drive to the Nauset Beach parking lot. From the parking lot, there is a marked path to Nauset Light.

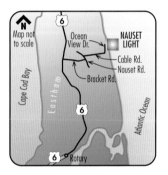

The new 48-foot white conical structure disassembled in Chatham, where it had been part of a twin-tower configuration, was planted on a concrete foundation inland from the existing signal, the last of a second trio of towers known as the Three Sisters. The last sister's legacy to its replacement was its fourth-order Fresnel lens and its 1875 Gothic Revival keeper's house.

The lighthouse, originally built in 1887, was painted red and white in 1940 to distinguish its day mark from surrounding navigational aids and to reflect the characteristic of its signal—alternating red and white flashes. In 1955, the beacon was automated. In 1981, its Fresnel lens, now on exhibit at the Salt Pond Visitor's Center in Eastham, was retired and succeeded by a DCB-224 Aerobeacon.

By 1993 the ever-receding precipice approached the cast-iron tower, and the U.S. Coast Guard proposed decommissioning the sea sentinel. The Nauset Light Preservation Society, however, managed to raise enough money to move the beacon 336 feet inland in 1997. A year later, the keeper's house was moved to its new location. Today, the beacon's light, shining 114 feet above sea level, is a private aid to navigation that can be seen for 20 miles.

Ned Point Light

Contact Information:
Bert Theriault
Lighthouse Keeper
E-mail: nedspointlight@attbi.com

Latitude: 41° 39' 06" N
Longitude: 70° 47' 48" W

After a tardy start, Ned Point Light began shining in 1837 on the northeast side of the entrance to Mattapoisett Harbor on Buzzards Bay. Faced with an unfinished project, the light's contractor, Leonard Hammond, whose holdings included a tavern, persuaded a building inspector to make an unscheduled sojourn to the builder's taproom before proceeding to the light. Meanwhile, Hammond's laborers hurried to make the light present-able. Their endeavors included laying planking over barrels where flooring should have been. During his examination, the inspector wandered too close

Ned Point Light

Mattapoisett, Massachusetts

Directions:
From New Bedford take I-195 north to exit
19. At the end of the ramp go right onto North
Street. Take North Street 1.3 miles to the end
and take a left onto Water Street. After 0.2
mile, Water Street becomes Beacon Street. Stay
straight on Beacon Street. After 0.3 mile bear
right onto Ned Point Road. Take Ned Point
Road 0.7 mile to the end at Ned Point and the
lighthouse. The tower is open during July and
August, Thursdays, 10 A.M. to noon. The
grounds are open to the public every day.

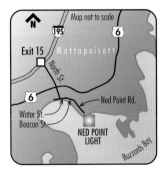

to the edge of the planking and fell into the
foundation. Unhurt physically, he emerged angry
and bereft of affection for Hammond.

The light's white, conical tower was built for $4,500 from rubblestone
gathered from a nearby beach. It is 39 feet high with a focal plane of 41 feet
and a range of 12 miles. The light's original hardware, 11 lamps with 13-
inch reflectors, was replaced with a fifth-order Fresnel lens in 1888. The
Fresnel was replaced with a plastic lens in 1961 and that lens replaced with
250-millimeter optics in 1996.

When the light was fully automated in 1923, the keeper's house was loaded
onto a barge and floated to Wings Neck Light in Bourne, Massachusetts. It
is said that the last keeper remained in the dwelling and cooked breakfast as
it was towed to its new location.

The U.S. Coast Guard decommissioned the light in 1952. Mattapoisett
gained ownership of the land surrounding the lighthouse in 1958. It built
an attractive park around the light, which was relighted in 1961 and is now
an active aid to navigation managed by U.S. Coast Guard Flotilla 67.

New Bedford Lightship

Latitude: N/A
Longitude: N/A

Contact Information:
City of New Bedford
133 William Street
New Bedford, Massachusetts 02740
Website: www.ci.new-bedford.ma.us

New Bedford Lightship

New Bedford, Massachusetts

Directions:
Take Interstate 195 to exit 15, Route 18.
Follow Route 18 to State Pier.

Anchored at the State Pier in New Bedford, the lightship LV114, also known as WAL-536, is a floating monument to the sailors who braved the sea's nastiest elements to guide their fellow mariners to safe waters. One of 15 remaining lightships, the vessel was built in 1930 at the Albina Iron Works in Portland, Oregon, for $228,121. The steel-hulled ship is 133 feet, 3 inches long, with a beam of 30 feet and a draft of 13 feet, 3 inches. Displacing 630 tons, the LV114 could average 9 knots with her 350 horsepower diesel electric motor. Essentially a floating lighthouse, the vessel had two 375-millimeter lanterns atop two 57-foot masts, as well as an air diaphone and hand-operated bell.

Upon completion, the lightship was assigned to the Fire Island station in New York. It made the voyage from Portland to New York through the Panama Canal in 46 days, with layovers, and was the first lightship to make the West Coast to East Coast trip. The vessel served at Fire Island until the station was closed in 1942. During World War II, the ship was used as an examination vessel. From 1945 to 1947, the craft was stationed at Diamond Shoal in North Carolina and later reassigned to the New England U.S. Coast Guard district, where it served as a relief vessel from 1947 to 1958. It regained a permanent station at Pollock Rip, Massachusetts, from 1958 to 1969, and later at Portland, Maine, from 1969 to 1971.

After the Coast Guard decommissioned the vessel in November 1971, it intended to use it as a floating maritime museum. Those plans, though, never developed, and the ship was transferred to New Bedford.

Newburyport Harbor Light

Latitude: 42° 48' 54" N
Longitude: 70° 49' 06" W

Contact Information:
The Friends of Plum Island Light, Inc.
P.O. Box 381
Newburyport, Massachusetts 01950
E-mail: YachtHarbor@aol.com

Newburyport, on the Merrimack River, was a significant seaport at the end of the 1700s. Shoals and shifting currents, however, made steerage in its harbor difficult, especially at the northern end of the neck of land known as Plum Island. After ad hoc measures by mariners to guide shipping headed up river proved inadequate, the state legislature authorized the building of two

Newburyport Harbor Light

Also known as Plum Island Light
Plum Island, Massachusetts

Directions:
From U.S. Route 95 north, take exit 57 to Storey Avenue. Take a right onto Storey Avenue then turn right onto High Street. Follow High Street and take a left onto Rolfes Lane. Follow Rolfes Lane to Plum Island Turnpike; turn right. Follow Plum Island Turnpike to Northern Boulevard; turn left. Follow Northern Boulevard to the lighthouse. The lighthouse grounds are accessible year-round. During the summer months, the light is occasionally open for tours. Check with the Friends of Plum Island Light (YachtHarbor@aol.com) for a tour schedule.

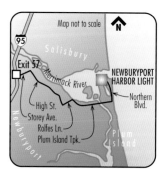

small wooden lighthouses in the area that were paid for with private funds and completed in 1788. The towers had movable foundations so they could be as mobile as the sandbars in the adjacent waters. The beacons acted as range lights. By lining up the lights, seafarers could find the best channel into the harbor.

In 1838, the original towers were replaced with two octagonal ones, also built on movable foundations. A small "bug light" was added to the station in 1855, and the next year, one of the octagonal towers was destroyed in a fire. It was never rebuilt, but the power of the remaining light was boosted by the installation of a fourth-order Fresnel lens.

Migrating sands forced the tower and bug light to be moved several times from 1870 to 1882. In 1898 the present 45-foot conical wooden tower, which stands 50 feet above sea level, was erected at the station, and the Fresnel was transferred to it. The light was electrified in 1927 and automated in 1951. In 1981, its characteristic was changed to flashing green. The U.S. Coast Guard did restoration work on the lighthouse in 1994 and 1997. Now the property of the city of Newburyport, the structure is cared for by the Friends of Plum Island Light.

Newburyport
Upper Range Front Light

Latitude: N/A
Longitude: N/A

Contact Information:
The Lighthouse
Preservation Society
4 Middle Street
Newburyport,
Massachusetts 01950
(800) 727-BEAM (2326)

Newburyport
Upper Range Rear Light

Newburyport Upper Range Lights

Newburyport, Massachusetts

Directions:
From U.S. Route 95 north, take exit 57 and turn right onto Storey Avenue. Take a right on High Street and then a left on Summer Street to Merrimac Street. Merrimac Street turns into Water Street. The rear range light is on the left. Beyond the rear range light is the U.S. Coast Guard station and the front range light.

Located 2 miles from the mouth of the Merrimack River, Newburyport, during its maritime heyday in the 18th and 19th centuries, needed help guiding shipping to its harbor and around the treacherous Goose Rocks. Help arrived in 1873 in the form of two lighthouses, a front range light and a rear range light. The front fanal was a white conical cast-iron affair, 14.5 feet high and located 25 feet above sea level. Three hundred fifty feet away, a 32-foot brick tower standing 47 feet above sea level served as the rear range light. Both towers were decommissioned in 1961.

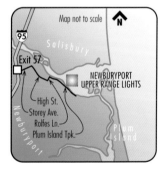

The height of the front light was about doubled around 1901, when it was capped with an octagonal wooden tower. Later, the lighthouse was raised to bring its height to 35 feet. In 1964, the light was toted to a nearby Coast Guard station. After being damaged by fire, the beacon was restored to its original configuration in 1990 with its restored lantern room resting atop the cast-iron tower. Restoration work on the light took place throughout the decade, spearheaded by the Lighthouse Preservation Society, which is headquartered in Newburyport, the birthplace of the U.S. Coast Guard.

The rear range light, its height boosted to 53 feet around 1901, was purchased by a private owner after its decommissioning. On occasion, the Society offers gourmet dinners at the top of the beacon.

Nobska Point Light

Latitude: 41° 30' 54" N
Longitude: 70° 39' 24" W

Contact Information:
Flotilla Commander Donald A. Abt
Woods Hole Flotilla 11-02
171 Sea Education Association
Woods Hole Road
Woods Hole, Massachusetts 02543
(508) 548-3307
E-mail: abtda@aol.com

The first navigational aid at Nobska Point, located at the entrance to Woods Hole Harbor, was constructed in 1828 for $2,249. Not only did it flag the harbor entrance, but it also cautioned ships of nearby danger at the Hedge Fence and L'Hommedieu shoals. Consisting of a lantern room atop the roof to the keeper's house, the signal was supplanted by the current tower in 1876.

Nobska Point Light

Woods Hole (Falmouth), Massachusetts

Directions:
Take Route 28 south to Falmouth, where it becomes Main Street. Take a right onto Shore Street and proceed to the end. Take a right onto Surf Drive to the split in the road. Bear left onto Oyster Pond Road to the intersection with Nobska Road. Take a left on Nobska Road and follow it to the lighthouse. Tours of the light are given on Thursdays and Saturdays from May to December by U.S. Coast Guard Auxiliary Flotilla 11-02.

The existing light is made of cast iron with a brick lining. It is 40 feet tall with a focal plane of 87 feet. Now painted white, its initial color was dark reddish-brown. A distinctive architectural detail of the beacon is the miniature brass lighthouse topping each baluster on its gallery.

Nobska Point's original optic was a fifth-order Fresnel lens swapped in 1888 for a brighter, fourth-order Fresnel with a range of 17 miles; still in use, it flashes white every 6 seconds with a red sector that makes the beacon appear crimson from the east. Its fog signal sounds two blasts every 30 seconds. Ancillary buildings include a Victorian keeper's house, constructed in 1876 and now serving as the headquarters for the group commander of the Woods Hole U.S. Coast Guard base, a brick oil house, a storage building, and a garage.

Although the Coast Guard took over management of the facility in 1939, civilian keepers staffed Nobska until 1972, when Joseph Hindley, reputedly the last civilian keeper in the United States, retired. The light was fully automated in 1985.

Nobska Point Light has been "adopted" by members of U.S. Coast Guard Auxiliary Flotilla 11-02. Member Payson A. Jones has been the "keeper" since 1996 and often greets visitors in a 19th-century keeper's uniform.

Palmer Island Light

Latitude: 41° 37' 36" N
Longitude: 70° 54' 36" W

City of New Bedford
133 William Street
New Bedford, Massachusetts 02740
Website: www.ci.new-bedford.ma.us

One would expect the seal of New Bedford to contain a likeness of a sperm whale, the leviathan on which the city built its early prosperity; yet equally prominent is one of the city's lighthouses, and so the seal shows Palmer Island Light, built during whaling's gravy days in 1849.

Palmer Island Light

New Bedford, Massachusetts

Directions:
Take Interstate 195 into New Bedford. Take
exit 15 for Route 18 south. Stay on Route 18
for 2 miles. Route 18 will become John F.
Kennedy Memorial Highway. Take a left onto
Potomska Street. Take a quick right onto
South Front Street. Go for 0.4 miles and take a
left onto Gifford Street, which will take you
behind some industrial buildings where you
can park and access the hurricane barrier. The
light is closed to the public except by special
arrangement, but it can be accessed at low tide
by the barrier.

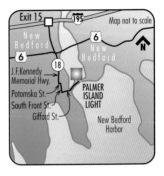

The 24-foot-high white conical tower with a black cast-iron lantern is
located at the northern end of Palmer Island in the Acushnet River west of
the entrance to New Bedford Harbor. Built of rubblestone—square- or
rectangular-cut stones that can be joined with a minimum of mortar—the
light has wooden windows and floors. Its lantern room, which is 4 feet high
and 7 feet in diameter, originally housed a fifth-order Fresnel lens, which
was replaced in 1999 with solar-powered optics. The beacon flashes white
for 2 seconds at 6-second intervals and can be seen for about 8 miles.

During the Hurricane of 1938, the keeper's house was destroyed, and the
keeper's wife, Mabel Small, was killed. Three years later, in 1941, the light
was fully automated. After the construction of the New Bedford hurricane
barrier, the light lost its usefulness to the U.S. Coast Guard and its operation
was discontinued in 1963. Ownership of the light changed hands several
times before New Bedford obtained the rights to the property in 1978. After
years of restoration work, the light was finally relighted on its 150th anniversary in August 1999.

Plymouth Light (The Gurnet)

Latitude: 42° 00' 12" N
Longitude: 70° 36' 00" W

**Contact Information:
Project Gurnet &
Bug Lights, Inc.
P.O. Box 2167
Duxbury,
Massachusetts 02331
Website: www.buglight.org**

As befits a lighthouse near "Plimoth Plantation," the station at Gurnet Point has several historic distinctions: It was the first station to have a lady lighthouse keeper (1790). It was America's first station with twin lights and is the nation's only lighthouse to have been pierced by a cannonball. Its south tower is the oldest freestanding wooden lighthouse in the United States.

The first twin lights were erected in 1768, built with £660 from the state legislature. The signals were raised at either end of the roof to the keeper's house.

During the Revolutionary War, a fort was built at the point. In 1776, a firefight broke out between the fort and a British frigate attempting to enter Plymouth Harbor. During the melee, a cannonball damaged one of the station's twin lights. Also that year, the light's first keeper, John Thomas, died of smallpox. John Thomas is best known as the major general who captured Dorchester Heights and forced the British to leave Boston. When the new federal government took control of the lighthouse in 1790, Hannah Thomas was appointed keeper, the first woman to hold such a position.

Fire razed the beacons in 1801, and in 1803 two 22-foot towers were constructed. They were 30 feet apart and cast a fixed white light 70 feet above sea level. By 1843, the beacons had fallen into disrepair and were replaced with

Plymouth Light (The Gurnet)

Plymouth, Massachusetts

Directions:
From Boston, take MA Route 3 south, which becomes the Southeast Expressway. As you approach the Braintree split (exit 7), stay in the left-hand lane. Merge onto exit 7, Route 3 south, Braintree/Cape Cod. Follow Route 3 to exit 11. Take exit 11, MA Route 14 east, Duxbury. At the exit's end, take a slight right onto MA Route 139/14/Congress Street. Stay on the route to the 139/14 split. Take a right onto Route 14. Follow Route 14, which will become St. Georges Street. Follow St. Georges Street to Washington Street. Take a left on Washington Street to Powder Point Avenue and turn right. Follow to Powder Point Bridge. Cross the bridge and park at the lot for Duxbury Beach. The lighthouse is a 4-mile hike along the Gurnet Peninsula.

Plymouth Harbor Cruises (800-242-2449), located at Town Wharf off Water Street, has cruises that offer scenic views of the Duxbury Pier Light, the Gurnet Point Light, the *Mayflower II*, and Plymouth Rock.

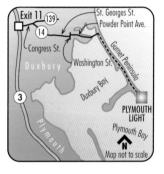

two 34-foot octagonal wooden towers. From the start, the towers' sixth-order Fresnel lenses were problematic and were often mistaken for lights from onshore housing. Although refitted with fourth-order Fresnels in 1871, the problem continued because the lights were so close together.

Nevertheless, both structures continued their careers until 1924, when the northeast tower was decommissioned and the south tower received a revolving beacon with a unique flashing sequence to set it apart from surrounding lighthouses. In 1998, the light was moved 140 feet inland to avoid destruction from erosion.

Point Gammon Light

Latitude: 41° 36' 35" N
Longitude: 70° 15' 58" W

Contact Information:
Private residence

Located at the southern end of Great Island in Yarmouth, Massachusetts, Point Gammon Light had an active life of only 40 years. The whitewashed fieldstone tower with a black lantern room was built in 1816. Architecturally unique among New England lighthouses, with its narrow windows and stonework, the tower resembles the keep of a medieval castle. Equipped with 11 oil lamps and reflectors, the 20-foot light shone a fixed white beam 70 feet above sea level for 13 nautical miles.

Point Gammon Light

Yarmouth, Massachusetts

Directions:

From Boston, take Route 3 south (Southeast Expressway) to Route 6 over the Sagamore Bridge to exit 6, Route 132. Take Route 132 into Hyannis. At the airport rotary, take the second right onto Barnstable Road. Follow Barnstable Road, which becomes Ocean Street after the intersection at Old Colony Road and South Street, to Kalmus Park. The lighthouse can be seen with binoculars from Dunbar Point within the park.

The signal marked the east side of Hyannis Harbor and the menacing rocks known as the Bishop and Clerks, located 2.5 miles from Point Gammon. The rocks are the remains of a five-acre island that was used for grazing sheep before it became submerged around 1750. Originally called Nantucket Shoals, the largest rock came to be known as the bishop and the surrounding rocks his "clerks." Similar nomenclature was used to name the craggy sea hazards 5 miles off St. David's Head in remote western Wales in Great Britain, which took the lives of the passengers and crew of the steamer *Nimrod* in 1860.

After the opening of a railhead in Hyannis in 1854, the port became extremely busy. In the year following the arrival of the railhead, for example, 4 steamboats, 216 brigs, 1,455 sloops, and 4,969 schooners plied by the light. Considered ineffective for handling that magnitude of traffic, the beacon was superseded with a lightship stationed at Bishop and Clerks until a lighthouse could be erected at that site. Bishop and Clerks Light was decommissioned in 1928 and razed in 1952.

Point Gammon Light has been a private residence since 1872. The keeper's house was dismantled in 1935 and the stone used to build a private butterfly museum on the island.

Portsmouth Harbor Light

Latitude: 43° 04' 18" N
Longitude: 70° 42' 30" W

Contact Information:
Friends of Portsmouth Harbor Lighthouse
P.O. Box 5592
Portsmouth, NH 03802-5092
(603) 431-9155
E-mail: FPHL@lighthouse.cc

Portsmouth Harbor Light

New Castle, New Hampshire

Directions:
From Route 95 north or south: Take exit 5 and follow signs to Route 1 Bypass South. Take Route 1 Bypass South. At the sixth traffic light, turn left onto Elwyn Road. Follow for approximately 1.4 miles and bear left to the stop sign. Turn left here; at about .5 mile take a right onto Route 1B. Cross the bridge and travel approximately 2 miles until you see signs for the Coast Guard Station Portsmouth Harbor and Fort Constitution. Follow to the parking area for Fort Constitution. You can see the lighthouse from the fort.

Established in 1771, Portsmouth Harbor Light was the first lighthouse north of Boston and the tenth lighthouse in America. The original beacon was wooden with a copper-roofed lantern and built on the premises of Fort William and Mary, notable as the fort of Paul Revere's infamous night ride.

Fort William and Mary eventually became Fort Constitution, and in 1793 President George Washington ordered that the light be staffed on a full-time basis. A second wooden beacon built in 1804 was replaced with a cast-iron tower in 1877, one of the first of its type to be built in New England. Portsmouth Harbor Light was electrified in 1934 and automated in 1960. Its original fourth-order Fresnel light, installed in 1877, still works as an active aid to navigation.

Race Point Light

Latitude: 42° 03' 48" N
Longitude: 70° 14' 36" W

Contact Information:
Race Point Lighthouse
P.O. Box 570
North Truro, Massachusetts 02652
(508) 487-9930
E-mail: racepointlighthouse@attbi.com

Named after a menacing crosscurrent outside the crook of Cape Cod whose victims included the ship-of-the-line HMS *Somerset* cited by William Wadsworth Longfellow in his poem "Paul Revere's Ride," the first Race Point Light was a 20-foot rubblestone tower built in 1816. The beacon, which was the third constructed on Cape Cod, was one of the first to use a revolving apparatus to create a flashing effect for its signal. That effect distinguished Race Point from nearby Highland Light.

A fog bell was added to the lighthouse in 1852. After the light was refitted with a fourth-order Fresnel lens in 1855, a brick building was raised in 1873

Race Point Light

Provincetown, Massachusetts

Directions:
Take U.S. Route 6 to Race Point Road in Provincetown. Take a right onto Race Point Road. Drive to the end of the road to the parking lot for Race Point Beach. From the parking lot, walk toward the U.S. Coast Guard station. A jeep trail leads from the station to the lighthouse. The walk is about 2 miles. Permits are needed to drive off-road vehicles on the beach and jeep trail. They can be obtained from the Cape Cod National Seashore or the Coast Guard station. Overnight accommodations are available at the light.

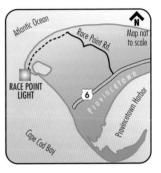

to house a steam-driven fog whistle. The following year, a second keeper's house was erected for assistant keepers and their families.

As the lime mortar between the bricks deteriorated over the years, the signal became increasingly leaky. To address that problem, the tower was resurfaced with wooden shingles in 1875. That proved to be a stop-gap measure, as the following year a new white conical tower, 45 feet tall and made of cast iron lined with brick, was built, as well as a new keeper's house. The Fresnel from the old light was transferred to the new one. In 1957, the lighthouse was converted to electricity and received a new, 1,000-watt lamp. In 1998, its optic was upgraded to a Vega solar-powered beacon.

The Gothic Revival keeper's house was demolished in 1960. At that time, the assistant keeper's house was renovated, and the light became part of the Cape Cod National Seashore. When the beacon was automated in 1978, the U.S. Coast Guard abandoned the assistant keeper's house, but it was renovated by the American Lighthouse Foundation in 1995 and has been used as an overnight guesthouse since 1997.

Sandy Neck Light

Contact Information:
Private residence

Latitude: 41° 43' 21" N
Longitude: 70° 16' 51" W

In the early 19th century, Barnstable, Massachusetts, was a bustling seaport for whalers, commercial anglers, and a thriving packet service to Boston. As the port grew, so did the need for a navigational aid to mark the entrance to the town's harbor. The first such aid was constructed for $3,500 in 1827 at the west end of the harbor at Sandy Neck. The lighthouse was a lantern room built atop a keeper's house made of brick. It emitted a fixed white light produced by 10 oil lamps, with reflectors, that shone 40 feet above sea level for a distance of 9 miles.

On the recommendation of a federal agency, a 40-foot conical white brick tower, which remains at the sight to this day, was built in 1857. It, too, exhibited a fixed white light from an oil lamp and a fifth-order Fresnel lens. In 1880, a new Gothic keeper's house was added to the site. By 1887, the tower began to show its age. At that time, two iron hoops and six staves were used to reinforce the fanal where cracks had appeared. The repairs can still be seen today.

Sandy Neck Light

Barnstable, Massachusetts

Directions:

From Boston, take Massachusetts Route 3 south (Southeast Expressway) to U.S. Route 6, which crosses Sagamore Bridge. After crossing the bridge, take exit 6, Massachusetts Route 132, toward Hyannis. At the first set of lights, turn left onto Phinney's Lane. Phinney's Lane becomes Hyannis Road. Follow Hyannis Road, which becomes Millway Road. Follow Millway Road to its end at the Millway Marina. A distant view of the light can be seen from Millway Beach, located near the marina. Binoculars are recommended.

To access the light by foot, take exit 4 off U.S. Route 6. At end of the exit, take a left onto Chase Road. Follow Chase Road to Old County Road. Take a right on Old County Road and follow it to Howland Lane. Turn left on Howland Lane. Follow Howland Lane to Route 6A. Turn left on Route 6A. Follow to Sandy Neck Road, take a right, and follow to end. The light is a 6-mile walk through Sandy Neck Conservation Area. Trail maps are available at cctrails.org.

Early in the 20th century, the Cape's ever-changing shoreline undermined the need for the lighthouse. It was decommissioned in 1931, and its Fresnel transferred to a new white skeletal steel tower some 200 feet closer to the ocean. Twenty-one years later, the skeleton tower was removed from service and supplanted with a lighted buoy flashing red every 2.5 seconds, warning ships of the shoals off Beach Point. At that time, the Sandy Neck light was "beheaded" and the property sold as surplus to private owners.

Sankaty Head Light

Contact Information:
The Sconset Trust, Inc.
15 McKinley Avenue
Siasconset, Massachusetts 02564
(508) 257-6610

Latitude: 41° 17' 00" N
Longitude: 69° 57' 54" W

Sankaty Head Light

Nantucket, Massachusetts

Directions:
From Nantucket center, follow Orange Street south to the rotary. From the rotary, take Milestone Road east to Siasconset and Sankaty Avenue. Take a left at Sankaty Avenue. Take a right at Emily Street. Take a left at Baxter Road and follow it to the lighthouse. The grounds, but not the tower, are open to the public.

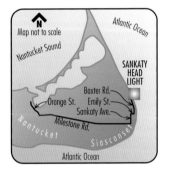

The treacherous shoals southeast of Nantucket sent shivers down the spines of sailors for more than 240 years before the resolve was obtained to build a lighthouse on the 90-foot bluff at Sankaty Head in Siasconset.

With a $12,000 appropriation from Congress, a brick keeper's house was erected in 1849, and a brick and granite 60-foot tower was completed the following year. The cylindrical beacon had a second-order Fresnel lens—the first light to use such hardware as original equipment—lighted by a single wick whale oil lamp. Its white beacon, visible for more than 27 miles, flashed twice for a minute and a half, followed by a 3-minute flare. So bright was the lighthouse that it became known as the Rocket Light or the Blazing Star. Always an island attraction, the platform opening below the lantern was widened in 1854 so that ladies with hoop skirts could better view the lantern's reflectors.

In 1888, the lantern room was replaced and the tower raised 10 feet, giving the light a focal plane of 158 feet. Electric lights were installed in 1933, and the signal's candlepower boosted sevenfold. The Fresnel (now on exhibit at the Nantucket Whaling Museum) was replaced in 1950 with a rotating beacon. Currently, the light has a DCB-224 Aerobeacon (installed in 1987) that flashes white every 7.5 seconds. The lighthouse, now white with a red band and black lantern, was automated in 1965. In 1994, all ancillary buildings were removed from the site by the U.S. Coast Guard. Threatened by erosion, efforts are underway to raise money to move the light farther inland.

Scituate Light

Latitude: 42° 12' 17" N
Longitude: 70° 42' 57" W

Contact Information:
Scituate Historical Society
Scituate, Massachusetts 02066
(781) 545-1083
Website: www.scituatehistoricalsociety.org

Scituate Light's shining moment came not from averting a maritime disaster but from thwarting a British raid during the war of 1812.

The 25-foot stone lighthouse, built in 1811, was barely three years old when, according to local lore, a British warship attempted to land a band of marauders on Scituate. At the time, the beacon was abandoned except for the keeper's daughters, Rebecca and Abigail. They spotted the Redcoats rowing toward shore but did not have time to spread the alarm. Instead, they took up fife and drum and began playing with vigor. Believing the music came from the local militia, the Brits turned tail, and the legend of the "Lighthouse Army of Two" was born.

Scituate Light

Scituate, Massachusetts

Directions:
From Boston, take MA Route 3 south (Southeast Expressway). As you approach the Braintree split (exit 7), stay in the left-hand lane. Merge onto exit 7, Route 3 south, Braintree/Cape Cod. Follow Route 3 to exit 13, Route 53 north. Follow Route 53 to Route 123 (Main Street). Follow Route 123 north to the intersection with Route 3A, about 6 miles. Cross over Route 3A. Route 123 becomes Country Way. Follow Country Way and turn right onto Stockbridge Road. Take a right at First Parish Road, then turn left onto Front Street and follow it to Jericho Road. Turn right at Jericho Road, follow to Lighthouse Road and turn right. Proceed to the parking lot. The keeper's house is a private residence. The tower is normally closed to the public, but there are open-houses each year.

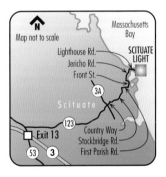

In 1827 a brick extension boosted the lighthouse's height by 15 feet. At the time, it displayed a fixed white light and a red light from windows located below the extension. Although the color scheme was designed to distinguish the signal from neighboring beacons, it proved largely ineffective, and vessels continued to be victimized by offshore ledges.

The first Minot's Ledge Light replaced the Scituate fanal in 1850, but a storm washed it out and the old beacon was pressed back into service in 1852. It received a new Fresnel lens in 1855, but when Minot Light was resurrected in 1860, Scituate station was darkened again.

In 1916, the federal government was prepared to dispose of the light, but Scituate intervened and purchased it. After a replica lantern was added to the tower in 1930, the site fell into disrepair, but it was enlivened in the 1960s due to efforts by the Scituate Historical Society. In 1989, funding was received to create a lighthouse park. By 1994, the signal was fully restored as a private aid to navigation, its white light visible 4 miles out to sea.

Stage Harbor Light

Latitude: 41° 39' 31" N
Longitude: 69° 59' 02" W

Contact Information:
Private residence

Like a specter from Sleepy Hollow, the headless Stage Harbor Light reposes on the barrier bar known as Harding Beach in Chatham, Massachusetts. As the commercial fishery perked up in Cape Cod waters at the end of the 19th century, Stage Harbor became a cozy hangout for deep-sea piscadors eschewing foul weather—especially after an 8-foot shipping channel was carved through the bar at Harding Beach. So in 1876, the Lighthouse Board of Trustees recommended that a lighthouse be constructed on the northeast side of the channel to guide ships safely through the famous "Chatham fog," a nightly occurrence during the summer months that makes the area one of the foggiest on the East Coast.

Stage Harbor Light

Chatham, Massachusetts

Directions:
From Boston, take Massachusetts Route 3 south (Southeast Expressway) to U.S. Route 6. Take Route 6 over the Sagamore Bridge to exit 9, Massachusetts Route 134. Take Route 134 toward Dennis–West Harwich. Follow Route 134 to Main Street. Turn left onto Main Street (Massachusetts Route 28) and follow for 8.7 miles to Barn Hill Road. Turn right onto Barn Hill Road. Follow to Hardings Beach Road and turn right. Drive to the beach parking lot at the end of the road. For a closer view, the private lighthouse is a 1-mile hike east of the beach parking area across the sand dunes. The lighthouse is private property. Please respect the privacy of the owners.

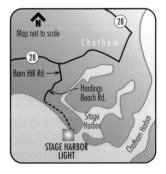

A 36-foot white conical tower made of curved iron plates lined with brick was erected at the site in 1880, as well as a two-story keeper's house. The pair was connected by a wooden walkway. It is said that during Prohibition, liquor was stored under the walkway's planking. Although the loose floorboards once caught an inspector's attention, his probe remained superficial, his only recommendation to the keeper being to nail down the boardwalk.

The light had a fourth-order Fresnel lens that shone a fixed white light 40 feet above sea level that could be seen for 12 nautical miles.

As a cost-saving measure, Stage Harbor Light was replaced in 1933 by a skeleton tower. At that time, the beacon's lantern room was removed, its tower capped, and the property sold as surplus to Henry Sears Hoyt, whose ancestors purchased the Chatham area from the Monomoyicks in 1656. Auxiliary buildings still standing at the site are the keeper's house, a boat shed, and an outhouse.

Straitsmouth Island Light

Latitude: 42° 39' 42" N
Longitude: 70° 35' 18" W

Contact Information:
Massachusetts Audubon Society
208 South Great Road
Lincoln, Massachusetts 01773
(781) 259-9500
Website: www.massaudubon.org

Straitsmouth Island Light

Rockport, Massachusetts

Directions:
Closed to the public, the light can best be seen by boat. Excursions offered by Cape Ann Cruises (978-283-1979) offer good views of the light. The Massachusetts Audubon Society occasionally organizes kayak trips to the island, but if you plan to hike on the key, bring plenty of calamine lotion as the topography is covered with poison ivy.

Straitsmouth Island's first aid to mariners was a 19-foot brick tower built in 1835. That beacon guided seafarers to nearby Pigeon Cove in Rockport, Massachusetts. Its first keeper, Benjamin Andrews, was chosen for reasons seemingly unrelated to his post: he was not likely to "serve as a juror, or to perform military duty."

Criticized by a lighthouse inspector as early as 1841 as a "specimen of contract work of the worst kind," the original structure was replaced by a 24-foot octagonal stone tower in 1850, which received a sixth-order Fresnel lens in 1857. In 1878, a one-and-a-half story Gothic keeper's house was built to quarter the lighthouse's caretakers. The wooden dwelling, which supplanted the original keeper's brick abode, remains on the atoll but is badly in need of repair.

The 1850 light was replaced by the present 37-foot white brick tower in 1896. In the 1960s, the entire island, save the lighthouse, was donated to the Massachusetts Audubon Society. When the fanal was automated in 1967, the Fresnel was swapped for a new optic. Currently, the active aid to navigation has a 250-millimeter solar-powered optic, which flashes green every 6 seconds 46 feet above sea level, and a foghorn that blasts once every 15 seconds when low visibility warrants it.

Tarpaulin Cove Light

Latitude: 41° 28' 08" N
Longitude: 70° 45' 24" W

Contact Information:
Cuttyhunk Historical Society
23 Tower Hill Road
Cuttyhunk, Massachusetts 02713
(508) 984-4611

Tarpaulin Cove Light

Naushon Island, Massachusetts

Directions:
The island is privately owned, but boaters are allowed access to the beach at Tarpaulin Cove and can then hike to the lighthouse. Private charter boats from New Bedford and Woods Hole make excursion trips in the vicinity of the light.

Naushon, the largest of the Elizabeth Islands—that 15-mile strip of keys that stretches southwest into Buzzards Bay from Woods Hole to Cuttyhunk—has long held welcome sights for sailors' eyes, as well as provided a safe harbor for pirates like Captain Kidd. In 1759, civic-minded tapmaster Zaccheus Lumbert built a beacon on the 5,000-acre island for the public good of whalers and coasters plying the bay. He paid for the upkeep of the signal out of his own purse, save for the whale oil given to him from time to time by the people of Nantucket.

Shipping volumes in the bay incited the federal government to buy land in 1817 at Tarpaulin Cove for a new lighthouse. Built of rubblestone, the first Naushon light was 38 feet tall with a focal plane of 71 feet. Its "birdcage" lantern room contained 10 lamps and shone a fixed, white signal. Those optics were replaced in 1856 with a fifth-order Fresnel lens from Paris.

After years of complaining by keepers, the original tower was supplanted by a new one, which, at 28 feet, was shorter than the old structure but was built on higher ground so its focal plane was greater, at 78 feet. The new white tower was made of brick and sported a brighter, fourth-order Fresnel. Another new addition was a 1,200-pound fog bell, which was later swept away by the Hurricane of 1938.

After the light was automated in 1941, its ancillary buildings fell into disrepair and were torn down in 1962. Its Fresnel lens has been replaced with a new 300-millimeter optic, which flashes white every 6 seconds and can be seen for 9 miles. The light is closed to the public and is best seen by boat.

Ten Pound Island Light

Latitude: 42° 36' 06" N
Longitude: 70° 39' 54" W

Contact Information:
First U.S. Coast Guard District
408 Atlantic Avenue
Boston, Massachusetts 02210-3350
(617) 223-8243

Legend has it that Ten Pound Island in Gloucester was named for the sum appropriated for its purchase from its Native American owners. It also garnered notoriety in the early 1800s as the haunt of a mysterious sea serpent with the head of a turtle.

The first light at Ten Pound Island was a 20-foot stone affair built, along with a keeper's house, in 1821. Despite complaints by some light keepers of shoddy construction throughout the signal's life, the lighthouse remained in

Ten Pound Island Light

Gloucester, Massachusetts

Directions:
The island is open to private boaters, but there is no landing facility except a small sandy beach. The lighthouse is not open to the public and is best seen by boat. The Gloucester Water Shuttle (978-804-9578) gives tours of the harbor that pass by the light, as does Cape Ann Cruises (978-283-1979). The lighthouse is clearly visible from many points along the Gloucester waterfront, including Fort Square. To reach Fort Square, take Route 128 to Route 127A. Follow Route 127A west to Commercial Street. Take a left onto Commercial Street. Follow Commercial Street to Fort Square.

service for 60 years. During the summer of its final year in service, Winslow Homer took up residence at the beacon and painted 50 canvases of Gloucester harbor.

The current light was first lighted in 1881. Although now white, the 30-foot conical cast-iron tower, which has a brick lining and foundation, was originally brown and equipped with a fifth-order Fresnel lens that has been replaced with a 250-millimeter optic. The original Fresnel can be seen at the Shore Village Museum in Rockland, Maine. Alternating between red and dark every 6 seconds, the beacon shines 57 feet above sea level. Its foghorn blasts twice every 20 seconds. Automated in 1934, the light was decommissioned in 1956 and suffered from neglect for many years. At the end of the 1980s, the Lighthouse Preservation Society of Newburyport, Massachusetts, and the city of Gloucester restored the signal over a two-year period at a cost of $45,000. The signal was relighted in 1989, when it once again became an active aid to navigation.

Three Sisters Lights

Contact Information:
Cape Cod National Seashore
(508) 255-3421
Website: www.nps.gov/caco/

Latitude: 41° 51' 34" N
Longitude: 69° 57' 36" W

Nauset Cliffs in North Eastham, Massachusetts, was the home of the first and only three-tower light station in America. The Three Sisters, as they came to be known, were built in 1838. The trio was created to distinguish it from Highland Light to the north and the Twin Lights (of Chatham) to the south. Erected on the cheap in 38 days, the winning bidder constructed the signals for $6,500—$3,500 less than what had been appropriated for the project. The threesome lasted until 1892, when erosion threatened the lighthouses. A second generation of sisters composed of three 29-foot wooden towers

Directions:
Take Massachusetts Route 3 south (Southeast Expressway) to Route 6 over the Sagamore Bridge. Continue on Route 6 to Eastham. At the third traffic signal from the Eastham/Orleans rotary, turn right onto Bracket Road. Drive to the end of Bracket Road and turn left onto Nauset Road. Follow Nauset Road to Cable Road. Turn right onto Cable Road. At the end of Cable Road, turn left onto Ocean View Drive and drive to the Nauset Beach parking lot. From the parking lot there is a marked path to Nauset Light. The Three Sisters is a short walk from Nauset Light.

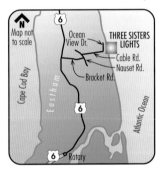

was raised farther inland. Later that year, the original Three Sisters tumbled into the sea, but occasionally the base of one of them can be seen from shore.

The cliffs continued to recede until, by 1911, their edge was only 8 feet from the northern tower. At that time, the authorities determined that one lighthouse was adequate for the site. The other two sisters were sold off for $3.50 and removed. The remaining signal was relocated farther inland. In memory of the Three Sisters, the beacon flashed three times every ten seconds.

Worn and shabby, the final sister was sold in 1923, just about the time it was decided to split up the duo known as the Chatham Twin Lights. One of the Chatham pair was moved to Nauset, where today it is a private aid to navigation.

The sisters were reunited by the National Park Service, which managed to repurchase the wooden towers between 1965 and 1975. By 1983, they were restored, although two sisters are "headless," and relocated in their original configuration—150 feet apart and 8.5 degrees off north—1,800 feet from the cast-iron tower.

West Chop Light

Latitude: 41° 28' 48" N
Longitude: 70° 36' 00" W

Contact Information:
Privately owned

West Chop Light

Vineyard Haven (Martha's Vineyard), Massachusetts

Directions:
Take Main Street from the ferry in Vineyard Haven to West Chop Road and the lighthouse. West Chop Light can also be seen from the ferries to Vineyard Haven.

The current lighthouse at West Chop on Martha's Vineyard is a sort of monument to the wisdom of zoning laws. Raised in 1891, the tower became a necessity when the opulent abodes of its affluent neighbors became a navigational hazard to shipping. By 1891, West Chop had become a playground for the rich; their homes were so large, they began to obscure the sight of the old lighthouse from the sea. The previous light, built in 1846, was located about 1,000 feet southwest of the first light at the site. That first light, which marks the entrance to Vineyard Haven Harbor

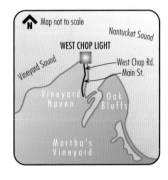

and the proximity of the dangerous Middle Ground Shoal, was a 25-foot rubblestone tower constructed for $5,000 in 1817. It sat on a bluff that by 1843 had eroded to within 37 feet of the edifice. To improve the 1846 beacon's visibility, a 17-foot mast topped with a light was added to the old lighthouse. Further extemporaneous additions proved unnecessary when the current cylindrical tower was erected. Initially painted red, it gave up its intense color for chaste white in 1896. Made of brick with a concrete and stone foundation, the current light is 45 feet tall with a focal plane of 84 feet. It's equipped with a fourth-order Fresnel lens, still used today, that is visible for 15 miles. It emits a white light with a red sector flashing every 4 seconds.

In 1976, West Chop was the last lighthouse on the Vineyard to become automated. An outstanding set of auxiliary buildings remains standing at the station—the keeper's house (1881), the fog signal building (1847), the oil house (1895), a storage building (1895), and a garage (1935)—together with the Vineyard Environmental Research Institute, which has played a pivotal role in preserving the island's lighthouses and uses the site for its offices.

West Dennis (Bass River) Light

Contact Information:
Lighthouse Inn
P.O. Box 128
1 Lighthouse Inn Road
West Dennis, Massachusetts 02670
(508) 398-2244
Fax: (508) 398-5658
E-mail: inquire@lighthouseinn.com

Latitude: 41° 39' 07" N
Longitude: 70° 10' 13" W

Billed by its owners as the only privately owned and maintained active aid to navigation in the nation, the Bass River Light is perched on the roof of the Lighthouse Inn in West Dennis, Massachusetts.

As the whaling industry increased shipping volumes in the ocean waters off Cape Cod, it also boosted traffic on inland waterways like the Bass River. In response, locals petitioned Congress in 1850 to establish a light to safeguard navigation in Nantucket Sound.

West Dennis (Bass River) Light

West Dennis, Massachusetts

Directions:
Take Route 28 to West Dennis. One-half mile from the Bass River bridge, turn right onto School Street then left onto Lower County Road. Follow it for 0.1 mile to Lighthouse Road and turn right. Follow for 0.3 mile, turn left onto Lighthouse Inn Road, and proceed to the inn.

Congress appropriated $4,000 for the lighthouse, which was completed in 1854. Materials were hauled by oxen across the nearby wetlands to build a one-and-a-half-story, white house with a conical iron tower and lantern room protruding from its roof 44 feet from the ground. First lighted in 1855, the beacon had a fourth-order Fresnel lens that shone a fixed white light for 12 nautical miles.

In 1880, the light was judged excess after a beacon was erected at Stage Harbor in Chatham. After Bass River Light was sold to private parties, the government was deluged with complaints. It repurchased the beacon and relighted it in 1881. With the opening of the Cape Cod Canal in 1914, sea traffic was diverted from the area. The Bass River Light was again extinguished and its Fresnel lens was removed.

Once more the light passed into private hands. It was expanded and converted into a summer home. In 1938, state senator Everett Stone bought the grounds with the intent of developing them. His plans were delayed, however, and in the interim, Stone's wife decided to open the building to lodgers to pay the property's mortgage until construction could begin. The venture proved so popular that the Stones decided to stay in the hospitality business.

In celebration of the 200th anniversary of the Lighthouse Service, the lighthouse was relighted in 1989 with a 300-millimeter optic that flashes white every 6 seconds.

Wings Neck Light

Latitude: 41° 40' 49" N
Longitude: 70° 39' 41" W

Contact Information:
Privately owned

Wings Neck Light

Bourne, Massachusetts

Directions:
From the rotary on the Cape Cod side of the Bourne Bridge take Route 28 south. Stay on Route 28 (General MacArthur Boulevard) for 3.4 miles, and then turn right onto Barlows Landing Road. Follow Barlows Landing Road for 2.1 miles, then take a right on Wings Neck Road. Stay on Wings Neck Road for 2.1 miles until you come to a cul-de-sac. The lighthouse is on private property with "No Trespassing" signs posted.

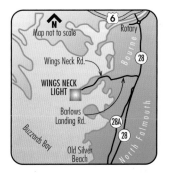

Wings Neck Light, in Pocasset, a village in Bourne, Massachusetts, not only has its own original buildings—an oil house constructed in 1849 and a keeper's house built in 1890—it has the beaconeer's home from Ned Point Light, built in 1870 and moved in 1922 to Wings Neck, a peninsula that extends into Buzzards Bay at the southwest end of the Cape Cod Canal. The dwellings are wood with fieldstone foundations.

In 1849, a Cape Cod-style house with a lantern room on the roof was established on Wings Neck. The lantern gave way to a fifth-order Fresnel lens in 1856. A fire damaged the structure in 1878, but the site remained operational until 1890. At that time, a handsome hexagonal pyramid, 33 feet tall with a focal plane of 50 feet, and a new keeper's house were constructed. In 1943, a steel tower was erected at the location to house a radar for the canal approach. After Cleveland East Ledge Light was erected in 1943, the beacon at Wings Neck lost its utility and was decommissioned in 1945. The light was sold to Frank and Irene Flanagan, of West Roxbury, Massachusetts, for $13,738 in 1947. The complex is not open to the public. It can best be seen from Scraggy Neck or by boat.

Wood End Light

Latitude: 42° 01' 18" N
Longitude: 70° 11' 36" W

Contact Information:
American Lighthouse Foundation
P.O. Box 889
Wells, Maine 04090
(207) 646-0245
E-mail: alf@lighthousefoundation.org

Although the Pilgrims extolled the sweet woods populating the land at the entrance to Provincetown Harbor, the navigational hazards in the nearby waters were no honeyed attraction for mariners. It was not until 1864, however, that the treacherous Wood End Bar and Shank Painter Bar received a day mark to warn seafarers away. That mark was replaced in 1872 with a 39-foot brick lighthouse and wooden one-and-a-half-story keeper's house built with a $15,000 appropriation from Congress. The tapered square structure was fitted with a fifth-order Fresnel lens that shone a flashing red

Wood End Light

Provincetown, Massachusetts

Directions:
The lighthouse can be viewed from the water from the Plymouth, Massachusetts, ferry and whale-watching excursions that leave from Provincetown Harbor. If you have a yen for adventure, though, you can make the trip to the light on foot. To do that, take Route 6 into Provincetown to Commercial Street (Route 6A). Take a left onto Commercial Street. Follow to the end of the street. Park at the breakwater. At low tide, you can hike on the half-mile-long breakwater to Wood End. The light is about a .75 mile walk along a sandbar to the right of the breakwater.

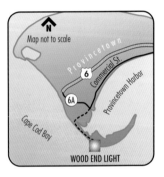

WOOD END LIGHT

light every 15 seconds, 45 feet above sea level that could be seen for 11 nautical miles.

In 1896, the light was converted to kerosene and an oil house was constructed, as well as a new wooden keeper's house and storage shed. Four years later, a revolving mechanism was built for the lighthouse's lens. Sound was added in 1902 when a pyramidal tower for a fog bell was erected. Since then, that signal has been replaced with an automated foghorn that bellows every 30 seconds during nasty weather.

Neither light nor bell could avert the disaster that occurred at the site on December 17, 1927. On that date, about a half mile south of the beacon, the U.S. Navy submarine *S-4* collided with the U.S. Coast Guard cutter *Paulding*. The sub was lost with all hands aboard.

Automation came to the lighthouse in 1961, and the U.S. Coast Guard demolished the keeper's house and storage shed. Subsequently, the beacon's original optic was replaced with a modern one. In 1981, the optic was converted to solar power.

Rhode Island Lighthouses

Conimicut Point Light

Although it may be small in size, Rhode Island has a surprisingly large number of lighthouses on its coastline. The "Ocean State" is home to twenty-one beacons, thirteen of which are active. In addition, visitors can view several former light stations where tower foundations are still visible. Included in this collection is the site of Lime Rock Light, which has since been converted to the Ida Lewis Yacht Club in Newport. Although a decorative light displayed seasonally is all that remains of this historic light station, the site has an intriguing history.

Idawalley Zoradia Lewis was a sixteen-year-old girl when her parents' health prevented them from their lightkeeping duties at Lime Rock Light. A strong swimmer, Ida assumed these duties with energy. Throughout her fifty-five years as keeper of Lime Rock Light, Ida is thought to have rescued as many as twenty-five mariners and became the most celebrated lighthouse keeper in American history. She made the covers of *Harper's Weekly* and *Frank Leslie's Illustrated Newspaper*, was the subject of the "Ida Lewis Waltz," and received a visit from United States President Ulysses S. Grant, who said, "I have come to see Ida Lewis, and I'd get wet up to my armpits if necessary."

While not listed in this publication, Lime Rock Light is a site that Rhode Island lighthouse lovers will not want to miss. The yacht club is not open to the public, but views are available of this and most other Rhode Island lighthouses from the many harbor cruises that are offered in the area.

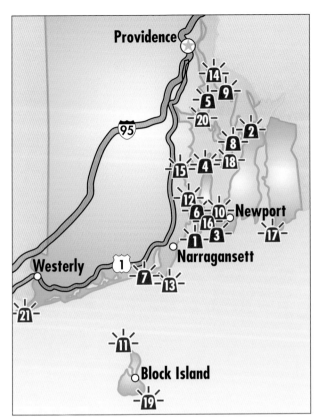

Rhode Island Lighthouse Locations by Number

Beavertail Lighthouse

Latitude: 41° 26' 58" N
Longitude: 71° 23' 59" W

Contact Information:
Beavertail Lighthouse
Museum Association
P.O. Box 83
Jamestown, RI 02835
Website:
www.beavertaillight.org

Beavertail Lighthouse is the third oldest lighthouse in America. Established in 1749 at the tip of Conanicut Island, the lighthouse replaced the bonfire and fog cannon that had served to mark the entrance to Narragansett Bay since 1705. The original 58-foot wooden tower burned down within a few years and was replaced in 1753 by a 64-foot stone beacon, fitted with a system of 15 lamps and reflectors. Tariffs on harbor use funded the upkeep of the tower in its early years, although expenses quickly surpassed the amount of income generated.

Beavertail Lighthouse

Jamestown, Rhode Island

Directions:
Beavertail Lighthouse may be reached via Route 138 from the east or west side of Narragansett Bay. After crossing the Jamestown Bridge (from North Kingstown) or the Newport Bridge (from Newport), follow the signs to Jamestown Center. Continue southward past Mackerel Cove Town Beach to Beavertail State Park at the tip of the island, where there is free parking. A view is also possible from the lighthouse cruises offered periodically by Bay Queen Cruises in Warren, Rhode Island. The cruise provides good views of a number of Narragansett Bay and Mount Hope Bay lighthouses. Call Bay Queen cruises at (401) 245-1350 or visit www.bayqueen.com for details. You can also see the lighthouse from trips offered aboard the sailing vessel *Mai Ling*; call (401) 965-5154 for details or visit the *Mai Ling* website at www.mai-ling.com.

Beavertail Lighthouse has a fascinating history. In 1817, the structure became the first lighthouse to be lit by gas, during an experiment by Newport inventor David Melville. Although gas proved to burn cleaner and brighter, opposition by the whale oil industry caused the government not to pursue usage of the new energy source. The British burned the lighthouse upon retreating from Newport Harbor in 1779, but President George Washington called for the lighthouse to be repaired and reactivated in 1790.

The current 45-foot granite structure was built in 1856 and was fitted with a third-order Fresnel lens. One year later, the nation's first steam-powered foghorn was added. Automated in 1972, Beavertail Lighthouse remains an active aid to navigation for the United States Coast Guard. The assistant keeper's house, built in 1898, has been converted into a historical museum and houses the beacon's fourth-order Fresnel, which was installed in 1975, but replaced by a modern rotating beacon in 1991.

Bristol Ferry Light

Latitude: 41° 38' 35" N
Longitude: 71° 15' 37" W

Bristol Ferry Light

Bristol, Rhode Island

Directions:
From RI 114 North or South: Travel until you reach the Mount Hope Bridge (toll) exit in Bristol. Turn east onto Ferry Road. Continue to a large turnaround. Parking is not permitted in the turnaround, so park on Ferry Road. You can view the lighthouse from the nearby rocky beach, but please remember to respect the privacy of the residents. You can also view Bristol Ferry Light from the lighthouse cruises offered periodically by Bay Queen Cruises in Warren, Rhode Island. The cruise provides good views of a number of Narragansett Bay and Mount Hope Bay lighthouses. Call Bay Queen cruises at (401) 245-1350 for details.

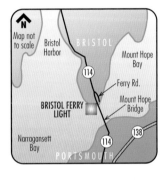

Although a private beacon had been maintained in the Narragansett Bay by the Fall River Steamboat Company since 1846, a petition to the Lighthouse Board by local ship captains prompted the construction of the Bristol Ferry Light at the entrance to Bristol Harbor in 1855. The 28-foot, white-brick, square tower, attached to a keeper's house, was positioned in the narrow passage between Mount Hope Bay and Narragansett Bay and was fitted with a sixth-order Fresnel that displayed a fixed white light visible for up to 11 miles at sea. It was first lit on October 4, 1855.

The light was upgraded to a fifth-order lens in 1902 and in 1916, the wooden lantern room was replaced by an iron version that was taken from a deactivated lighthouse. The tower was also raised 6 feet during its time of service.

In 1927 the lighthouse was decommissioned and replaced by a steel skeleton tower, which in turn was replaced by the Mount Hope Bridge in 1929. Since 1929, Bristol Ferry Light has been privately owned. It can be viewed from the north side of the Mount Hope Bridge, along with the original 1855 keeper's house and 1904 oil house.

Castle Hill Lighthouse

Latitude: 41° 27' 42" N
Longitude: 71° 21' 48" W

Castle Hill Lighthouse

Newport, Rhode Island

Directions:
In Newport, take America's Cup Avenue and Thames Street (one way) to Wellington Avenue and turn right. Turn left at Halidon Avenue, then right onto Harrison Avenue. Turn right onto Castle Hill Road, then left onto Ocean Drive. Turn right at a paved road with a small "Inn at Castle Hill" sign. Turn right to the Castle Hill Cove Marina and park there. The lighthouse is reached via a quarter-mile trail that begins opposite the marina entrance. It leads over a hill and to concrete steps leading to the lighthouse. You can also see the lighthouse from trips offered aboard the sailing vessel *Mai Ling*, call (401) 965-5154 for details or visit the *Mai Ling* website at www.mai-ling.com.

Congress first proposed the establishment of a lighthouse on Castle Hill in 1875, but construction was halted for several years due to the opposition of noted Harvard professor and naturalist Alexander Aggasiz, who argued that the beacon would encroach on his property. While waiting for the dispute to be resolved, steamboat companies painted the rocky cliffs of Castle Hill white to serve as a marker. In 1886, Aggasiz finally relented and sold his property on Castle Hill to the government.

The 34-foot granite structure was first lit on May 1, 1890 and was fitted with a fifth-order Fresnel lens and a fog bell. Its style has been described as "Richardsonian Romanesque," a term that refers to famed architect H.H. Richardson, who is thought to have helped design Castle Hill Lighthouse.

The upper half of the all-gray tower was painted white in 1899. Castle Hill Lighthouse was automated in 1957 and continues to exhibit a flashing red light across Narragansett Bay as an active aid to navigation today. The light is not open to the public, but the grounds are accessible and are just a short walk from the Castle Hill Inn.

Conanicut North Light

Latitude: 41° 34' 24" N
Longitude: 71° 22' 18" W

Conanicut North Light

Jamestown, Rhode Island

Directions:
From RI 138 in Jamestown, take East Shore Road north. At the northern tip of the island, where East Shore turns west, turn right into a dirt road. The lighthouse is about one tenth of a mile from the turn.

The square, wooden tower and six-room Gothic Revival-style keeper's quarters that serve as Conanicut North Light were built in 1886 to help mari-

ners navigate the dangerous north point of Conanicut Island. The black lantern was originally fitted with a fifth-order Fresnel lens that displayed a fixed white light, but a new optic with a fixed red light was substituted in 1907.

In 1933, Conanicut North Light was replaced by an automatic light on a steel skeleton tower, which was discontinued altogether in the 1980s. The original lighthouse was sold at auction and is now privately owned. The tower has since been painted red with white trim, and the lantern house has since been removed and capped. Along with the tower, the lighthouse's original 1897 barn and 1901 brick oil house still stand.

Conimicut Point Light

Latitude: 41° 43' 00" N
Longitude: 71° 20' 42" W

Conimicut Point Light

Warwick, Rhode Island

Directions:
Conimicut Point Light can be seen from
Conimicut Point Park in Warwick. From I-95
North or South: Take exit 13 to the Airport
Access Road. Follow the road onto RI 117 (West
Shore Road). The road eventually becomes Bush
Avenue. Turn left at Symonds Avenue, then right
at Point Avenue and follow to the park. The park
is open year-round, sunrise to sunset, but there is
a parking fee from July to Labor Day. Conimicut
Point Light can also be seen from the area
around Nayatt Point in Barrington, and a good
view is possible from the lighthouse cruises
offered periodically by Bay Queen Cruises in
Warren, Rhode Island. The cruise provides good
views of a number of Narragansett Bay and
Mount Hope Bay lighthouses. Call Bay Queen
cruises at (401) 245-1350 for details.

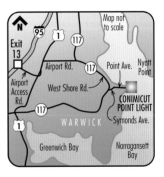

The 58-foot lighthouse that marks Conimicut Point Shoal today is the
second lighthouse to be built in this location. The first, a granite tower with
no accompanying keeper's dwelling, was constructed in 1868. Until 1882,
when an updated tower was built on the spot, keepers resided at the nearby
discontinued Nayatt Point Lighthouse and rowed to Conimicut Point to
tend to the lighthouse.

The new lighthouse built at Conimicut Point was designed in the sparkplug
style of Connecticut's Stamford Harbor Light, with living quarters built into
the structure. A fourth-order Fresnel lens exhibited a fixed white light and a
red sector was added later. In 1960 Conimicut Point Light was the last
American lighthouse to become electrified; three years later, the beacon
became automated as well. Conimicut Point still serves as an active aid to
navigation under the auspices of the United States Coast Guard.

Dutch Island Lighthouse

Latitude: 41° 29' 48" N
Longitude: 71° 24' 16" W

Contact Information:
Dutch Island
Lighthouse Society
P.O. Box 40151
Providence,
Rhode Island 02940

Dutch Island became a major trading center in the 1630s as the West India Company bartered novelties in exchange for furs, meat, and fish from the Indians. As traffic increased in the area, the government allocated funds for a lighthouse to mark the west passage of Narragansett Bay that led to Dutch Island Harbor.

Dutch Island Lighthouse

Jamestown, Rhode Island

Directions:
Dutch Island Lighthouse can be viewed from the Fort Getty Recreation Area in Jamestown. Eastbound on RI 138: Cross over the Jamestown Bridge and continue to an exit just west of the Newport Bridge, marked with a "Jamestown" sign. Westbound on RI 138: Cross over the Newport Bridge to the Jamestown exit. Then follow Wolcott Avenue south; turn right at Hamilton Avenue, then left at Southwest Avenue to the entrance to the Fort Getty Recreation Area. There are day fees and camping fees in the park, though you may be allowed a free short stay if you state that your purpose is to visit the lighthouse. Follow the loop road around the park until it reaches the high ground by the bay with a view of Dutch Island.

The first lighthouse built here in 1826 was constructed of stones from the island. A 42-foot brick tower and keeper's house were built here in 1857 and the light was fitted with a fourth-order Fresnel lens. Gun batteries built during the Civil War years were expanded in the twentieth century and became a military camp known as Fort Greble. Men stationed at this fort in 1923 noticed a fire that had gotten out of hand at Dutch Island Lighthouse and stopped the blaze from destroying the beacon.

In 1924, the fixed white light was changed to a flashing red signal and automated in 1947. Frequent vandalism to the abandoned beacon prompted the Coast Guard to discontinue the light in the 1970s, and in 1979, Dutch Island Lighthouse was sold to the state of Rhode Island.

In 2000, the Dutch Island Lighthouse Society was formed to restore the historic beacon. The group is raising funds and accepting donations for a complete renovation of the Dutch Island Lighthouse, which has been recognized as a national historic landmark. The tower, though not open to the public, is currently part of the Bay Islands State Park.

Gooseberry Island Light

Latitude: 41° 23' 07" N
Longitude: 71° 31' 08" W

This privately owned stone, aluminum, and glass structure was built over a period of five years and completed in 1999. It stands 35 feet tall and is topped by a lantern room that overlooks Gooseberry Island's marshes and ponds and the Atlantic Ocean.

The lighthouse was the brainstorm of John Hooper, a retired football coach and inventor from New Jersey who has always been drawn to lighthouses. He began pursuing his dream of owning his own "toy" beacon over a decade ago, when he and his family bought a piece of property in Snug Harbor and filed for a permit.

Gooseberry Island Light

Wakefield, Rhode Island

Directions: This lighthouse is privately owned and not open to the public. It is best seen from the water. Southland Cruises in Galilee offers a ride aboard the *Southland Riverboat* that has an excellent view of the lighthouse. Call (401) 783-2954 for details. Gooseberry Island Light can also be seen from Snug Harbor Marina in Wakefield, Rhode Island.

After much research, Hooper began working on a model of the structure and an attached replica seventeenth-century cottage. Hooper and his family began collecting rocks from old construction sites and Hooper himself used an electric winch to position and mortar the stones.

Companies in Rhode Island, Maine, and Texas were hired to provide the different parts of the lighthouse, including the spiral staircase and aluminum frame to hold the windows above the stone walls. The lantern room, the most intricate part of the project, was constructed in Galilee, Rhode Island, by Jay and David Gallup of Rhode Island Engine. Hooper and his daughter-in-law, engineer Kimberly Hooper, worked with the Gallups using computer-assisted-design technology to create the final design. The Gallups then welded the industrial-strength diamond-plate aluminum to match the blueprints and delivered it in 1999.

Although United States Coast Guard regulations prevent the Hoopers from installing a beacon in the tower, the family plans to furnish the lighthouse with maritime antiques, including an authentic telescope, ship's wheel, and binnacle.

Hog Island Shoal Light

Latitude: 41° 37' 54" N
Longitude: 71° 16' 24" W

Hog Island Shoal Light

Portsmouth, Rhode Island

Directions:
From RI 114 south: You can see the lighthouse offshore to the right as you cross the Mount Hope Bridge. Just after crossing the bridge, turn right onto a cloverleaf interchange. Circle around to Bristol Ferry Road and turn left. Cross a set of railroad tracks. Drive straight ahead to the old ferry wharf. From RI 114 north: Drive straight ahead onto Bristol Ferry Road as you approach the Mount Hope Bridge. The view is fairly distant; bring your binoculars. A good view is also possible from the lighthouse cruises offered periodically by Bay Queen Cruises in Warren, Rhode Island. The cruise provides good views of a number of Narragansett Bay and Mount Hope Bay light-houses. Call Bay Queen cruises at (401) 245-1350 for details.

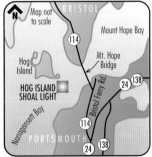

A privately owned lighted ship marked this dangerous spot in the east passage of the Narragansett Bay for twenty years before it officially became established as a light station. In 1886, the 72-foot Hog Island Shoal Lightship was officially stationed at the south end of the island to mark the shoals surrounding Bristol Harbor.

The last lighthouse to be built in Rhode Island, Hog Island Shoal Light was built in 1901 to replace the lightship. The 60-foot, cast-iron structure was supported by a series of caissons and designed in the sparkplug style that was popular at the time. The black lantern atop the white tower was fitted with a fifth-order Fresnel lens, which was upgraded to a fourth-order Fresnel in 1903. Hog Island Shoal Light was automated in 1964, and its 250-millimeter optic continues to welcome mariners to the bay with a six-second intermit-tent flashing white light.

Nayatt Point Lighthouse

Latitude: 41° 43' 31" N
Longitude: 71° 20' 20" W

Nayatt Point Lighthouse

Barrington, Rhode Island

Directions: Nayatt Point Lighthouse can be seen from Barrington Town Beach. The beach is open only to residents of Barrington in the summer, but is open to everyone in the off-season. A good view is also possible from the lighthouse cruises offered periodically by Bay Queen Cruises in Warren, Rhode Island. Call Bay Queen cruises at (401) 245-1350 for details.

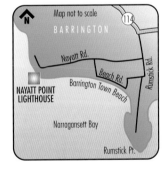

Nayatt Point Lighthouse was constructed in 1828 to assist mariners in navigating past treacherous Conimicut Point. The 23-foot brick tower was not built well and suffered much damage in an 1855 storm. The decision was made to rebuild and the current 25-foot, square tower was erected in 1856.

In 1868, a lighthouse was built at Conimicut Point and effectively put Nayatt Point Lighthouse out of service. Nayatt Point Lighthouse continued to serve as keeper's quarters, however, as the new beacon at Conimicut Point was not built with a living area. Eventually a new Conimicut Point Light was built with keeper's quarters, and the Nayatt Point Lighthouse was sold at auction to a private owner in 1890. The 1828 house, Rhode Island's oldest keeper's quarters, is privately owned. The lighthouse is still operational and fitted with a lantern from a former lightship, but it is not currently used as a navigational aid.

Newport Harbor Light

Contact Information:
The American Lighthouse Foundation
P.O. Box 889
Wells, Maine
(207) 646-0515
www.lighthousefoundation.com

Latitude: 41° 29' 36" N
Longitude: 71° 19' 36" W

Newport Harbor Light

Also known as Goat Island Light
Newport, Rhode Island

Directions:
From RI 114 South in Newport: Turn right at Admiral Kalbfus Road. Then turn left at Third Street, then right at Sycamore Street (one way). Turn left at Washington Street, then turn right at the Goat Island Connector. Park at the Hyatt Hotel. The grounds of the lighthouse are accessible by passing through the lobby of the hotel. A good view is also possible from the lighthouse cruises offered periodically by Bay Queen Cruises in Warren, Rhode Island. Call Bay Queen cruises at (401) 245-1350 for details. Several other cruises in Newport offer views of the lighthouse, including M/V *Amazing Grace*, (401) 847-9109; *Spirit of Newport*, (401) 849-3575; Viking Tours of Newport, (401) 847 6921; and Yankee Boat Peddlers, (800) 427-9444.

Goat Island, primarily used as a military base for much of the nineteenth century, is home to Newport Harbor Light. A lighthouse was first established on the south end of the island in 1823, but it soon became evident that the location was ineffective and the light was too dim. In 1842, a new breakwater was built on the north end of the island and equipped with a 35-foot octagonal granite lighthouse. The original lighthouse was moved to Prudence Island, where it still stands.

A fourth-order Fresnel was installed in 1857 and exhibited a fixed green light visible for up to 11 nautical miles. A keeper's house was added to the new light in 1865 and a fog bell was added to the structure eight years later. Newport Harbor Light was electrified in 1922, one year before the keeper's house was damaged by a naval torpedo boat and demolished.

Today the light, which was automated in 1963, is located adjacent to the grounds of the Hyatt Regency Newport and can be accessed by walking through the hotel. Since 2000, the Newport Harbor Light has been leased by the American Lighthouse Foundation.

North Light

Latitude: 41° 13' 42" N
Longitude: 71° 34' 36" W

North Light Fund
P.O. Box 1183
Block Island, Rhode Island
02807
Website:
www.angelfire.com/stars/
richardrrg/
TheNorthLightFund.htm

Block Island, a popular Rhode Island vacation spot, has also been the site of several shipwrecks. The frequent fog and dangerous shoals in the area have been the source of trouble for many mariners over the years. Between 1819 and 1839, 59 vessels were stranded or wrecked on the island.

A lighthouse was first commissioned on the sand bar known as Sandy Point in 1829. Known as Sandy Point Light, the 45-foot granite structure with twin beacons was threatened by erosion due to its unstable location. A second twin light was built in 1837 further inland, but this light was found to be ineffective due to its distance from the shore. Sandy Point Light was rebuilt as a single tower in 1857, but again fell victim to erosion.

North Light

Block Island, Rhode Island

Directions:
Block Island can be reached by ferry from Point
Judith, Rhode Island; New London, Connecticut; and Montauk, New York. For information
on the Point Judith and New London ferries call
Interstate Navigation at (401) 783-4613. For
information on the Montauk ferry, call Viking
Fleet Ferry Lines at (516) 668-5700. You can
also fly to Block Island via New England Airlines
from Westerly (RI) Airport; call (800) 243-2460
for information. Block Island North Light is a
few miles from the ferry landing. Bicycle rentals
are available and taxis are usually in the vicinity
of the ferry. If you bring your car: leave the ferry
and turn right on Water Street. Follow onto
Dodge Street. Turn right at Corn Neck Road
and follow to the free parking area at the end of
the road. The lighthouse is about a .05-mile
walk on the sandy beach.

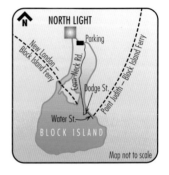

In 1867, North Light, affectionately known as "Old Granitesides," became
the fourth light to be built on Sandy Point. Unlike the previous towers,
North Light was built with a solid concrete foundation to avoid the forces of
erosion. The two-and-one-half-story, Victorian-style keeper's quarters and
iron tower was built 700 yards inland and fitted with a fourth-order Fresnel
that exhibited a fixed white light visible from 13 miles at sea. The optic was
later changed to a flashing white light and was electrified in the 1940s.

Although deactivated in 1973 and replaced with an offshore skeleton
tower, North Light remained a popular tourist attraction for Block Island
visitors. The area became part of a wildlife refuge known for its flourishing
bird community. Residents soon began to petition for a relighting of the
beacon and North Light was reactivated on August 5, 1989. The lighthouse now serves as an active aid to navigation and a museum. Plans are
underway to restore the upper floors of the lighthouse and convert the
light to wind power.

Plum Beach Light

Latitude: 41° 31' 49" N
Longitude: 71° 24' 19" W

**Contact Information:
The Friends of Plum
Beach Lighthouse, Inc.
P.O. Box 451
Portsmouth, RI 02871**

Plum Beach Light

North Kingstown, Rhode Island

Directions:
Travel west on RI 138 in Jamestown and take the exit marked North Main Street. Turn left at Frigate Street, and left again at Beacon Street. Turn right at Pickering Street, left at Helm Street, and right at Spindrift Street. The lighthouse can be seen from the end of Spindrift Street. A good view is also possible from the lighthouse cruises offered periodically by Bay Queen Cruises in Warren, Rhode Island. Call Bay Queen cruises at (401) 245-1350 for details.

Plum Beach Light, built in the west passage of the Narragansett Bay, was built at the request of ship captains who detoured Dutch Island in dense fog. Due to the stormy weather and choppy water in the area, the caisson-supported tower was a challenge to construct and was not completed until June 1899. In the meantime, a temporary red lantern and fog bell were installed to guide ships traveling in the area.

The 53-foot white conical tower was first fitted with a fourth-order Fresnel that flashed a white beam every five seconds. Plum Beach Light survived several severe winters and, more impressively, the Hurricane of 1938, which destroyed many Rhode Island lighthouses and killed 262 people in the area.

In 1941, upon completion of the Jamestown Bridge, Plum Beach Light was rendered obsolete and decommissioned. For several years, the lighthouse suffered neglect as the U.S. Coast Guard and the state of Rhode Island argued about who owned the structure. In 1998, the government ruled that the state owned the light. One year later, the property was purchased by the nonprofit group The Friends of Plum Beach Lighthouse, who began restoration on the lighthouse in the summer of 2002. Restoration was completed in 2003, and the refurbished light is now a private aid to navigation.

Point Judith Lighthouse

Latitude: 41° 21' 42" N
Longitude: 71° 28' 54" W

Although a formal lighthouse was not built on this spot until 1810, a day beacon had been installed at the busy shipping harbor of Point Judith before the American Revolution to mark the mile-long shoal that protrudes from the Rhode Island coast between Block Island Sound and Narragansett Bay.

The original light at Point Judith, built of wood at a cost of $5,000, was destroyed in an 1815 storm. A 35-foot granite lighthouse with a revolving light replaced the original the following year. Unfortunately, shipwrecks continued to occur in the area, and the lighthouse was demolished and replaced with the current 51-foot brownstone tower in 1857.

Point Judith Lighthouse

Narragansett, Rhode Island

Directions:
From US Route 1 in Wakefield, take the exit for RI 108 south to Point Judith. The road terminates at a four-way stop. Turn right onto Ocean Road and follow to the light station. The grounds are open daily and there is free parking.

In 1931, Point Judith Lighthouse made history when it became the first station in Rhode Island to have a radio beacon, which allowed vessels to navigate at night or in stormy weather without relying on the light or foghorn to guide them. The octagonal structure, equipped with a fourth-order Fresnel lens that exhibits a flashing white light, continues to serve Point Judith's busy harbor today, although the light was automated in 1954. A U.S. Coast Guard station was built adjacent to the lighthouse in 1937, and while the 1857 keeper's house has been demolished, the light's original 1917 oil house and 1923 fog-signal building still stand.

Point Judith Lighthouse underwent a major restoration in the summer of 2000, when the Coast Guard spent approximately $250,000 renovating the historic tower and lantern room. Visitors can walk the refurbished light's grounds today, although the lighthouse itself is not open to the public.

Pomham Rocks Lighthouse

Latitude: 41° 46' 36" N
Longitude: 71° 22' 12" W

The light at Pomham Rocks, named for a Narragansett Indian chief who fought in King Philip's War and was killed in 1676, was first lit on December 1, 1871. The two-story, French Second Empire-style house was built with an adjoining light tower that held a sixth-order Fresnel lens.

A fog siren was added in 1900. Local residents, however, complained of the continuous noise and the horn was replaced three years later by a fog bell. In 1939, Pomham Rocks Light's sixth-order Fresnel was upgraded to a

Pomham Rocks Lighthouse

East Providence, Rhode Island

Directions:
Pomham Rocks Lighthouse can be easily seen from the East Bay Bicycle Path in East Providence. The path is open to walkers as well as bikers. It extends from Bristol to Providence. To reach the parking area closest to the lighthouse: Head east on I-195, take exit 4, Riverside/Veteran's Memorial Parkway (RI 103). Continue about 5 miles to the Bullocks Point Road parking area to reach the bike path. The view of the lighthouse is a short walk to the north.

fourth-order lens, which was subsequently removed upon the lighthouse's decommission in 1974 and put on display at the Custom House Maritime Museum in Newburyport, Massachusetts.

Pomham Rocks Light was sold to the neighboring Mobil Oil Company in 1980. Although the light is no longer functional, it is still cared for by the energy giant and can be viewed from the East Bay Bicycle Path.

Poplar Point Light

Latitude: 41° 34' 16" N
Longitude: 71° 26' 21" W

Poplar Point Light

Wickford, Rhode Island

Directions:
Poplar Point Light is best viewed from across Wickford Harbor at Sauga Point. From US Route 1 in Wickford, take Camp Avenue south. Turn right at Shore Acres Road. On Shore Acres there is a pathway marked with a "Private Property" sign. The path is actually a public walkthrough. Head down the lane to the beach, then walk west to a breakwater. From the breakwater, Poplar Point Light can be seen across the harbor.

The 48-foot wooden tower known as Poplar Point Light served as a navigational aid at the entrance of Wickford Harbor for only half a century. Built in 1831 for $3,000, the wooden, Cape Cod-style light originally held a series of eight lamps and 14.5-inch reflectors, which were replaced in 1855 by a fifth-order Fresnel lens.

In 1882, Poplar Point Light was put out of service by the more powerful Wickford Harbor Light. Poplar Point Light is the oldest surviving lighthouse in Rhode Island still on its original site, and it is believed to be the oldest original wooden lighthouse in the United States. The structure has been privately owned since 1894.

Rose Island Lighthouse

Latitude: 41° 29' 42" N
Longitude: 71° 20' 36" W

Contact Information:
Rose Island Lighthouse Foundation
P.O. Box 1419
Newport, Rhode Island 02840-0997
(401) 847-4242
www.roseislandlighthouse.com

This French Second Empire Revival-style lighthouse was built at the corner of Rose Island in 1870 to help mariners navigate the tricky east passage of Narragansett Bay. Before construction of the light, steamboat companies sent a man on a rowboat out to the spot to sound a fog signal in stormy

Rose Island Lighthouse

Newport, Rhode Island

Directions:
Rose Island Lighthouse can be seen distantly from various points on shore. The island is reached via the Jamestown-Newport ferry. The roundtrip fare is $12 for adults, and $6 for children between the ages of six and ten. Children must be accompanied by an adult. The ferry stops at Rose Island on request, and there is a $1 landing fee per person. The ferry leaves Goat Island Marina in Newport. Call (401) 423-9900 for ferry information. Rose Island Light can also be viewed from several harbor tours leaving Newport, including M/V *Amazing Grace*, (401) 847 9109; *Spirit of Newport*, (401) 849-3575; Viking Tours of Newport, (401) 847-6921; and Yankee Boat Peddlers, (401) 847-0298 or (800) 427-9444.

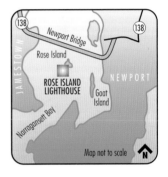

weather as a warning to approaching vessels. Rose Island Lighthouse's sixth-order Fresnel lens was first lit on January 20, 1870 and exhibited a fixed red light. A fog bell was added fifteen years later.

Rose Island was part of the Naval Torpedo Station in the twentieth century, and explosives were stored in the island's partially built Fort Hamilton during World War I and World War II. After the second world war, the military sold its property on the island and abandoned the area. This left it open to vandalism, which became worse in 1971 when the Newport bridge was built and Rose Island Lighthouse was decommisioned.

After a stint as a marine research station for the University of Rhode Island, Rose Island Lighthouse was purchased by a group of citizens who formed the Rose Island Lighthouse Foundation. In 1984, the group took over the historic property and began to restore it to its former glory. On August 7, 1993, Rose Island Lighthouse was relit. Guests who want a true taste of "keeper life" can reside at the lighthouse for overnight or weeklong stays. During these visits, guests raise the flag, record the weather and other data, and perform general maintenance chores.

Sakonnet Point Lighthouse

Contact Information:
The Friends of Sakonnet Point
Lighthouse, Inc.
P.O. Box 154
Little Compton, Rhode Island

Latitude: 41° 27' 12" N
Longitude: 71° 12' 12" W

Sakonnet Point Lighthouse

Sakonnet, Rhode Island

Directions:
Travel south on RI 77 in Tiverton until you reach its terminus near the beach in Little Compton. There is a free parking area. On the left, just before the beach parking area, walk down a narrow paved lane to a walled beach overlook. In summer, the beach is open to residents only, but you can see the lighthouse from the overlook, about six-tenths of a mile away.

On the east side of the Sakonnet River is Little Cormorant Rock. It is here that Sakonnet Point Lighthouse was established in October 1884, after nearly a year of construction. The white, conical lighthouse equipped with a fourth-order Fresnel lens is Rhode Island's easternmost beacon. Over the years, the 66-foot tower weathered many storms, including the Hurricane of 1938 and Hurricane Carol in 1954. Though no keepers were ever injured as a result of the storms, the powerful elements took their toll on the brick-lined iron tower.

Sakonnet Point Lighthouse was decommissioned in 1954 and sold to a private owner at auction. In 1985, the lighthouse was donated to The Friends of Sakonnet Point Lighthouse, Inc., a nonprofit organization dedicated to raising funds for the restoration of the beacon. After extensive renovation, the tower was equipped with a modern optic that exhibits a red flash every six seconds and was relit on March 22, 1997.

The light continues to serve as an active aid to navigation and can be seen up to seven miles at sea.

Sandy Point Lighthouse

Latitude: 41° 36' 36" N
Longitude: 71° 18' 12" W

Contact Information:
Prudence Conservancy
P.O. Box 115
Prudence Island, Rhode Island 02872

Sandy Point Lighthouse

Also known as Prudence Island Lighthouse
Prudence Island, Rhode Island

Directions:

Prudence Island can be reached via car/passenger ferry (crossing time is about 20 minutes) from Bristol's Church Street Wharf. From RI 114 in Bristol, take any cross street to Thames Street. The wharf is at the intersection of Thames and Church Streets. Call (401) 253-9808 for ferry information. From the ferry dock on Prudence Island, the lighthouse is approximately a 1-mile walk. Head left from the ferry dock. There are no restaurants on Prudence Island, so plan accordingly. The lighthouse can also be viewed from the occasional lighthouse cruises offered by Bay Queen Cruises in Warren, Rhode Island. Call Bay Queen cruises at (401) 245-1350 for details.

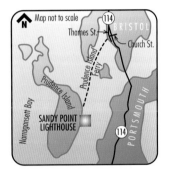

Sandy Point Lighthouse originally stood on Newport Harbor's Goat Island. The 25-foot granite tower was relocated to Sandy Point, located on Prudence Island, in 1851 and lit in 1852. A fifth-order Fresnel replaced the beacon's earlier lighting system in 1857 and a fog bell was added in 1885. Sandy Point Lighthouse was upgraded to a fourth-order Fresnel in 1939 and electrified. Twenty-two years later, the structure was automated.

The keeper's house was destroyed in one of the worst disasters in the lighthouse's history. During the Hurricane of 1938, the building was swept away, killing keeper George Gustavus's wife, son, and three others. Gustavus himself was swept into the sea, but was carried back onto shore moments later. After the storm, Gustavus resigned from his post as keeper and never returned to the lighthouse.

Sandy Point Lighthouse still serves as an active aid to navigation and is now fitted with a 250-millimeter modern lens. The light, though not open to the public, is accessible to visitors who take a ferry from Bristol. The lighthouse is approximately a 1-mile walk from the ferry port.

Southeast Light

Contact Information:
Block Island Southeast
Lighthouse Foundation
Box 949
Block Island, RI 02807
(401) 466-5009

Latitude: 41° 09' 12" N
Longitude: 71° 33' 06" W

Southeast Light, the highest light in New England, was built as an accompaniment to Block Island's North Light. In 1856, the government issued $9,000 for the construction of a lighthouse at the southeast tip of Block Island. The money was instead used to repair the existing North Light and Southeast Light was forgotten until 1872, when a local merchant started a petition to have a lighthouse built on the spot. T.H. Tynan of State Island served as the construction company for the Italianate/Gothic Revival-style light.

The completed light was one of the grandest in the nation, with an attached brick keeper's house standing tall at two-and-a-half stories. Other buildings included a garage, a storage building, a boathouse, and an oil house. The octagonal tower was installed with a first-order Fresnel lens, which was first lit on February 1, 1875.

Southeast Light

Block Island, Rhode Island

Directions:

Block Island can be reached by ferry from Point Judith, Rhode Island; New London, Connecticut; and Montauk, New York. For information on the Point Judith and New London ferries call Interstate Navigation at (401) 783-4613. For information on the Montauk ferry, call Viking Fleet Ferry Lines at (516) 668-5700. You can also fly to Block Island via New England Airlines from Westerly (RI) Airport; call (800) 243-2460 or (401) 596-2460 for information. Block Island Holidays offers a wide range of tour packages and activies on the island; call (800) 905-0590 or (401) 466-3115. From the ferry, walk to the road and turn left; Block Island Southeast Light is about a 30-minute walk (some of it uphill). Taxis are readily available in the area near the ferry.

In 1929, the light was changed to a flashing green beacon to help sailors differentiate it from other lights in the area. During the Hurricane of 1938, which wrecked the house's radio beacon and oil house and destroyed all power connections, keepers were forced to turn the lens by hand for several days. The present electric fog signal was added in 1974.

In 1990, the Coast Guard deactivated the light and replaced it with a steel skeleton tower. Over the years, erosion had crept up on the light, leaving it standing a mere 55 feet from the edge of the island. The light soon was on the National Trust for Historic Preservation's list of most endangered historic structures. Thanks to a group of volunteers who started the Block Island Southeast Lighthouse Foundation, the light was moved in August 1993 to its current location about 300 feet from the edge of the bluffs. The group restored the light and efforts to relight the beacon were rewarded on August 27, 1994.

Southeast Lighthouse is now home to a small museum and gift shop. Tours of the structure are available throughout the summer.

Warwick Light

Latitude: 41° 40' 00" N
Longitude: 71° 22' 42" W

Warwick Light

Warwick, Rhode Island

Directions:
From US Route 1 North: Turn right onto RI 117, then right again at Warwick Neck Avenue. Continue south to the light station. Visitors are not admitted into the station, and the view from the gate is partly blocked. A good view from the water is available from the lighthouse cruises offered periodically by Bay Queen Cruises in Warren, Rhode Island. Call Bay Queen cruises at (401) 245-1350 for details.

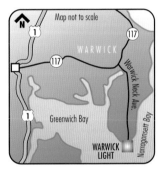

Warwick Light was first established in 1826. The 30-foot tower was originally attached to the roof of a two-room stone building. The house's keeper complained that the house was too cramped and damp, and the original house was replaced with a three-room wooden house in 1831. The new quarters were replaced with a Victorian dwelling in 1889 and the former wooden keeper's house was converted to a barn.

In 1932, the lighthouse was torn down after years of being threatened by erosion and a new 51-foot steel tower with an electric light was built on the site. This beacon flashes a green beam every four seconds and continues to serve as an active aid to navigation for the United States Coast Guard.

Watch Hill Lighthouse

Contact Information:
Watch Hill Lighthouse
Keepers Assocation
14 Lighthouse Road
Watch Hill, RI 02891

Latitude: 41° 18' 12" N
Longitude: 71° 34' 30" W

Watch Hill Lighthouse

Westerly, Rhode Island

Directions:
From RI 1A North or South: Turn south onto Watch Hill Road, which will eventually bear slightly right onto Wauwinnett Road. Bear left onto connecting Bay Street. Turn left at Larkin Road. Just before Bluff Road on the right is Lighthouse Road; a paved lane leads to the lighthouse station. Seniors (64+) and the handicapped are permitted to drive to the parking area near the station. Others must park outside of Lighthouse Road and walk to the lighthouse.

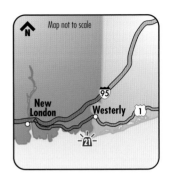

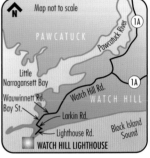

Watch Hill Tower receives its name from the watch tower and beacon that were established here as early as 1745. The decision to build a lighthouse here to mark the eastern entrance to Fishers Island Sound was approved in 1806 by President Thomas Jefferson.

The first beacon on the spot was a 35-foot, round, wooden tower with ten whale oil lamps and reflectors. Erosion eventually threatened the tower and a new structure was built further inland in 1856. The new tower was 45 feet tall and lined with brick. Its fourth-order Fresnel lens emitted a fixed white light. A two-story keeper's house and protective sea wall were also built during this time.

After the steamer *Metis* sunk near Watch Hill in 1872, killing over 100 passengers, a United States Life Saving Service Station was established near the lighthouse. The station was abandoned in the 1940s and demolished in 1963.

In 1986, Watch Hill Lighthouse became automated and the Fresnel lens was replaced with a modern optic. Watch Hill Lighthouse continues to serve as an active aid to navigation and today is home to a museum that is open to the public for limited hours in the summer. The light's original fourth-order Fresnel lens is on display in the museum. Watch Hill Lighthouse is run by the Watch Hill Lighthouse Keepers Association, which is in charge of the station's upkeep. The group has hired a resident keeper for the light.

Appendix

EDITOR'S NOTE: The following information was confirmed at press time. We recommend, however, that you call the appropriate numbers to confirm lodging, attraction, and event information before traveling.

2004 Massachusetts Calendar of Events

March   Greater New Bedford Half Marathon, New Bedford
(508-998-5068)

April   Annual Daffodil Festival, Nantucket (508-228-1700,
www.nantucketchamber.org)

May   Nantucket Wine Festival, Nantucket (508-228-1128,
www.nantucketwinefestival.com)
Essex River Race, Essex (978-281-2642 or 978-774-5077,
www.blackburnchallenge.com)

June   Historical Society of Old Newbury Annual Garden Tour,
Newburyport (978-462-2681, www.newburyhist.com)
Rockport Chamber Music Festival, Rockport (978-546-7391)
Swan Festival, Wareham (508-291-3677, www.warehamvillage.com)

July   New Bedford Summerfest & Blessing of the Fleet, New Bedford
(508-999-5231, www.newbedfordsummerfest.com)
Newburyport Yankee Homecoming, Newburyport
(978-462-9253, www.yankeehomecoming.com)
Annual Swim Buzzards Bay, New Bedford
(508-999-6363, www.savebuzzardsbay.org)

August   Newburyport Yankee Homecoming, Newburyport
(978-462-9253, www.yankeehomecoming.com)
Gloucester Waterfront Festival, Gloucester (978-283-1601)
Sandcastle and Sculpture Day, Nantucket
(508-228-1700, www.nantucketchamber.org)
Outdoor Arts and Crafts Fair, Wareham (508-295-1501)

September   Gloucester Schooner Festival, Gloucester (978-283-1601)
Around the Cape Ann Road Race (25k), Cape Ann (978-283-0470)
Bourne Scallop Festival, Buzzards Bay (508-759-6000)
Harwich Cranberry Festival, Harwich
(508-430-2811, www.harwichcranberryfestival.com)

October   Salem Haunted Happenings, Salem
(978-744-3663 or 877-SALEM-MA, www.hauntedhappenings.org)

December   Annual Christmas Stroll Weekend, Nantucket
(508-228-1700, www.nantucketchamber.org)

Beverly (Hospital Point Range Rear)
Other Sites of Interest:
John Hale House, Beverly (978-922-1186)
Beverly Historical Society & Musuem, Beverly (978-922-1186)
Montserrat College of Art Galleries, Beverly (978-921-4242)
Sedgwick Gardens at Long Hill, Beverly (978-921-1944)

Accommodations:
Beverly Farms Bed & Breakfast Inn, Beverly (978-922-6074)
Gordon's 1841 House Bed & Breakfast, Beverly (978-921-2612 or 888-927-2612)

Buzzards Bay (Buzzards Bay Entrance Tower)
Other Sites of Interest:
The National Marine Life Center, Buzzards Bay (508-743-9888, www.nmic.org)
Cape Cod Central Railroad, Hyannis and Sandwich
(508-771-3800 or 888-797-RAIL, www.capetrain.com)

Accommodations:
The Beachmoor Inn & Restaurant, Buzzards Bay
(508-759-7522, www.beachmoor.com)
A Hillview Bed and Breakfast, Buzzards Bay
(508-888-0214 or 877-888-0219, www.ahillviewbnb.com)
Bay Motor Inn, Buzzards Bay (508-759-3989)
Buttermilk Bay Inn, Buzzards Bay
(508-743-0800 or 877-592-3242, www.buttermilkbayinn.com)

Gloucester (Eastern Point, Ten Pound Island, Dog Bar, Annisquam)
Other Sites of Interest:
Yankee Whale Watch & Deep Sea Fishing, Gloucester
(800-WHALING, www.yankeefleet.com)
The Sargent House Museum, Gloucester (978-281-2432, www.sargenthouse.org)
Schooner *Adventure*, Gloucester (978-281-8079, www.schooner-adventure.org)
Hammond Castle Musuem, Gloucester (978-283-7673, www.hammondcastle.org)

Accommodations:
Gray Manor Bed & Breakfast, Gloucester
(978-283-5409: summer; 321-784-8766: winter)
The Inn at Babson Court, Gloucester (978-281-4469, www.babsoncourt.com)
Lanes Cove House, Gloucester (978-282-4647, www.lanescovehouse.com)

New Bedford (Clark's Point, New Bedford Lightship)
Other Sites of Interest:
New Bedford Whaling Museum, New Bedford (508-997-0046)
Rotch-Jones-Duff House & Garden Museum, New Bedford (508-997-1401)
New Bedford Art Museum, New Bedford (508-961-3072)
Buttonwood Park Zoo, New Bedford (508-991-6178, www.bpzoo.org)
New Bedford Whaling National Historical Park, New Bedford (508-996-4095)

New Bedford (Clark's Point, New Bedford Lightship) *cont.*
Accommodations:
Holiday Inn Express Fairhaven-New Bedford, New Bedford (508-997-1281)
Comfort Inn New Bedford/Dartmouth, North Dartmouth
(508-996-0800 or 800-228-5150, www.comfortinndartmouth.com)
Edgewater Bed & Breakfast, Fairhaven (508-997-5512)

Newburyport/Plum Island (Newbury Point Front Range Tower, Newburyport Rear Range Tower, Newburyport Harbor)
Other Sites of Interest:
Firehouse Center for the Performing and Visual Arts, Newburyport (978-462-7336, www.firehousecenter.com)
Maudslay Arts Center, Newburyport (978-499-0050)
Cushing House Museum, Newburyport (978-462-2681)
Custom House Maritime Museum, Newburyport (978-462-8681)
Spencer-Peirce-Little Farm, Newbury (978-462-2634, www.spnea.org)

Accommodations:
Essex Street Inn, Newburyport (978-465-3148, www.essexstreetinn.com)
Newburyport Bed & Breakfast, Newburyport
(978-463-4637, www.newburyportbedandbreakfast.com)
Walton's Ocean Front, Plum Island (978-465-7171, www.waltonsoceanfront.com)
Garrison Inn, Newburyport (978-499-8500, www.garrisoninn.com)

Rockport (Cape Ann Light Station on Thacher Island, Straitsmouth Island)
Other Sites of Interest:
Halibut Point State Park, Rockport (978-546-2997)
Paper House, Rockport (978-546-2629)
Essex River Cruises & Charters, Essex (800-748-3706, www.essexcruises.com)

Accommodations:
Yankee Clipper Inn, Rockport
(978-546-3407 or 800-545-3699, www.yankeeclipperinn.com)
Beach Knoll Inn, Rockport (978-546-6939 or 866-546-6939, www.beachknoll.com)
Emerson Inn By the Sea, Rockport
(978-546-6321 or 800-964-5550, www.emersoninnbythesea.com)
The Inn on Cove Hill, Rockport
(978-546-2701 or 888-546-2701, www.innoncovehill.com)
Old Farm Inn, Rockport (978-546-3237 or 800-233-6828, www.oldfarminn.com)
Pleasant Street Inn, Rockport
(978-546-3915 or 800-541-3915, www.pleasantstreetinn.net)

Wareham (Nantucket Lightship)
Other Sites of Interest:
Cartland, Wareham (508-295-8360)
Nantucket Whaling Musuem, Nantucket (508-228-1736, www.nha.org)
Water Wizz (water park), Wareham
(508-295-3255: in-season; 401-364-2070: off-season; www.waterwizz.com)
Fearing Tavern Musuem, Wareham (508-295-6839)

Accommodations:
Harbor Watch Inn, Onset (508-295-4600, www.harborwatchinn.com)
Atlantic Motel, Wareham (508-295-0210)
Onset Village Inn By the Sea, Onset (508-273-0700, www.onsetvillageinn.com)
Centre Street Inn, Nantucket (508-228-0199, www.centrestreetinn.com)
Le Languedoc Inn & Bistro, Nantucket (508-228-4298, www.lelanguedoc.com)

2004 New Hampshire Calendar of Events

April	Annual Quilt Show, Plaistow (978-688-1688)
May	5K Road Race and Children's Fun Run, Portsmouth (603-436-3853, www.childrens-museum.org) Rye By the Sea Duathlon and Road Race, Rye (603-431-7867, www.ryebythesea.org)
June	Master Sand Sculpting Competition, Hampton Beach (603-926-8718, www.hamptonbeach.org) Market Square Day, Portsmouth (603-436-3988, www.proportsmouth.org)
July	Tommy Gallant/Seacoast Jazz Festival, Portsmouth (603-436-2848, www.artfest.org) Exeter Revolutionary War Festival, Exeter (603-772-2622, www.independencemuseum.org) New England 300, Loudon (603-783-4931, www.nhis.com) Stratham Fair, Stratham (603-772-4977, www.strathamfair.com) All British "Show of Dreams" Auto Show, Portsmouth (603-422-7552, www.strawberybanke.org)
September	Seafood Festival, Hampton Beach (603-926-8718, www.hamptonbeachseafoodfestival.com)
October	Apple Harvest Day, Dover (603-742-2218, www.dovernh.org)
December	Candlelight Stroll, Portsmouth (603-422-7552, www.strawberybanke.org)

Accommodations in New Hampshire

Portsmouth (Isles of Shoals Light)
Other Sites of Interest:
The Children's Museum of Portsmouth, Portsmouth
(603-436-3853, www.childrens-museum.org)
Smuttynose Brewing Co., Portsmouth (603-436-4026, www.smuttynose.com)
Strawbery Banke Museum, Portsmouth (603-433-1100, www.strawberybanke.org)

Portsmouth (Isles of Shoals Light)

Accommodations:

The Governor's House, Portsmouth (866-427-5140, www.governors-house.com)
The Inn at Strawbery Banke, Portsmouth
(800-428-3933, www.innatstrawberybanke.com)
Martin Hill Inn, Portsmouth (603-436-2287)
The Port Inn, Portsmouth (800-282-PORT, www.theportinn.com)
Sise Inn, Portsmouth (877-747-3466, www.siseinn.com)

Rye/New Castle (Portsmouth Harbor Light)

Other Sites of Interest:

The Seacoast Science Center, Rye (603-436-8043, www.seacentr.org)

Accommodations:

Arbor Inn Bed and Breakfast, Rye (603-431-7010, www.arborinn.com)
Rock Ledge Manor Bed & Breakfast, Rye (603-431-1413)
Wentworth by the Sea, New Castle Island (866-240-6313, www.wentworth.com)

2004 Rhode Island Calendar of Events

January	Jamestown Penguin Plunge, Jamestown (401-823-7411, www.gonewport.com)
February	Newport Winter Festival, Newport (401-847-7666, www.newportevents.com)
March	Irish Heritage Month, Newport (401-845-9123, www.gonewport.com) Home Show at the Rhode Island Convention Center, Providence (401-458-6000, www.ribahomeshow.com) St. Patrick's Day Parade, Newport (401-845-9123, www.gonewport.com)
April	Pawtucket Red Sox Opening Day, Pawtucket (401-724-7300, www.pawsox.com) Newport Kids Fest, Newport (401-845-6608, www.gonewport.com) Easter Egg Hunt, Newport (401-846-1398, www.gonewport.com) Daffodil Days, Bristol (401-253-2707, www.blithewold.org) Earth Day, Bristol (401-245-7500, www.asri.org) Pawtucket River Duck Race, Westerly (401-596-7761, www.westerlychamber.org)
May	WalkAmerica Newport 2004, Newport (401-454-1911) Fort Adams Opening Day, Newport (401-841-0707, www.fortadams.org) Chorus of Westerly Spring Concert (401-596-8663, www.chorusofwesterly.org)

May	Newport Spring Boat Show, Newport (401-846-1115, www.newportexhibition.com) "Virtu" Art Festival, Westerly, (401-596-7761, www.westerlychamber.org) Gaspee Days Arts and Crafts Festival, Warwick (401-781-1772, www.gaspee.com)
June	Festival of Historic Houses Candlelight Tour, Providence (401-831-7440, www.ppsri.org) Newport International Film Festival, Newport (401-846-9100, www.newportfilmfestival.com) Snug Harbor June Moon Madness Striper Tournament, Wakefield (401-783-7766, www.snugharbormarina.com) Gaspee Days Parade, Warwick (401-781-1772, www.gaspee.com) Rhode Island National Guard Open House and Air Show, North Kingstown (401-275-4110, www.riguard.com) Narragansett Art Festival, Wakefield (401-783-1820, www.wakefieldrotary.com) Sunset Musical Festival, Newport (401-846-1600, www.newportfestivals.com)
July	Sunset Musical Festival, Newport (401-846-1600, www.newportfestivals.com) Bristol Fourth of July Parade, Bristol (401-253-0445, www.July4thbristolri.com) Campbell's Hall of Fame Tennis Championships, Newport (401-849-6053, www.tennisfame.com) Snug Harbor Shark Tournament, Wakefield (401-783-7766, www.snugharbormarina.com) Wickford Art Festival, North Kingstown (401-294-6840, www.wickfordart.org) Black Ships Festival, Newport (401-847-7666, wwww.newportevents.com)
August	Newport Folk Festival, Newport (401-847-3700, www.newportfolk.com) Narragansett Indian Pow Wow, Charlestown (401-364-1100, www.narragansett-tribe.org) JVC Jazz Festival, Newport (401-847-3700, www.festivalproductions.net) Fools' Rules Regatta, Jamestown (401-423-1492, www.jyc.org)
September	Classic Yacht Regatta and Parade, Newport (401-847-1018, www.moy.org) Rhythm and Roots Festival, Charlestown (888-855-6940, www.rhythmandroots.com) Newport International Boat Show, Newport (401-846-1115, www.newportboatshow.com) Jonnycake Storytelling Festival, South Kingston (401-789-9301) Aquafina Taste of Rhode Island, Newport (401-846-1600, www.newportfestivals.com)

October	Block Island Birding Weekend, Block Island
	(401-949-5454, www.asri.org)

October	Block Island Birding Weekend, Block Island (401-949-5454, www.asri.org) Jack O'Lantern Spectacular, Providence (401-785-3510, www.rwpzoo.com) Scituate Art Festival, North Scituate (www.scituateartfestival.org) NBC-10 International Oktoberfest, Newport (401-846-1600, www.newportfestivals.com) Woonsocket Autumnfest, Woonsocket (401-762-9072, www.autumnfest.org) Brooks Pharmacy Ocean State Marathon, Warwick to Providence (401-885-4499, www.oceanstatemarathon.com) Bowen's Wharf Seafood Festival, Newport (401-849-2120, www.bowenswharf.com) RIIFF Horror Film Festival, Providence (401-861-4445, www.film-festival.org)
November	Fine Furnishings, Providence (401-841-9201, www.finefurnishingsshow.com) Guy Fawkes Bonfire, Misquamicut (401-596-9441, www.misquamicut.org) Christmas at the Newport Mansions, Newport (401-847-1000, www.newportmansions.org) Christmas in Newport, Newport (401-849-6454, www.christmasinnewport.org) Festival of Lights, North Kingstown (401-295-5566) Christmas at Blithewold, Bristol (401-253-2707, www.blithewold.org)
December	Christmas at the Newport Mansions, Newport (401-847-1000, www.newportmansions.org) Christmas in Newport, Newport (401-849-6454, www.christmasinnewport.org) Festival of Lights, North Kingstown (401-295-5566) Christmas at Blithewold, Bristol (401-253-2707, www.blithewold.org) First Night Newport (401-848-2400, www.firstnightnewport.org)

Accommodations in Rhode Island

Barrington (Nayatt Point)
Other Sites of Interest:
Bay Queen Cruises, Warren (401-245-1350)
Blithewold Mansion and Gardens, Bristol (401-253-2707)
Haffenreffer Museum of Anthropology, Bristol (401-253-8388)
Mount Hope Farm, Bristol (401-254-1745)
Preservation Society Museum, Barrington (401-247-3770)

Accommodations:
Bristol Harbor Inn, Bristol (401-254-1444)

Candlewick Inn, Warren (401-247-2425)
Hearth House, Bristol (401-253-1404)
Nathaniel Porter Inn, Warren (401-245-6622)
Thomas Cole House, Warren (401-245-9768)

Block Island (North, Southeast)
Other Sites of Interest:
Block Island Historical Society, New Shoreham (401-466-2481)
Manisses Animal Farm, New Shoreham (401-466-2421)
Rodman's Hollow, New Shoreham (401-466-2129)

Accommodations:
The 1661 Inn and Hotel Manisses, New Shoreham (401-466-2421)
Harbourview Cottages, New Shoreham (401-466-2807)
Hygeia House, New Shoreham (401-466-9616)
The National Hotel, New Shoreham (401-466-2901)
Rose Farm Inn, New Shoreham (401-466-2034)

Bristol (Bristol Ferry)
Other Sites of Interest:
Audubon Society of Rhode Island's Environmental Education Center, Bristol (401-245-7500)
Blithewold Mansion and Gardens, Bristol (401-253-2707)
Haffenreffer Museum of Anthropology, Bristol (401-253-8388)
Herreshoff Marine and America's Cup Museum, Bristol (401-253-5000)
Mount Hope Farm, Bristol (401-254-1745)

Accommodations:
Bradford Dimond Norris House, Bristol (401-253-6338)
Bristol Harbor Inn, Bristol (401-254-1444)
Point Pleasant Inn, Bristol (401-253-0627)
Rockwell House Inn, Bristol (401-253-0040)
William's Grant Inn, Bristol (401-253-4222)

East Providence (Pomham Rocks)
Other Sites of Interest:
Crescent Park Looff Carousel, East Providence (401-433-2828)
Governor Henry Lippitt House Museum, Providence (401-453-0688)
Providence Athenaeum, Providence (401-421-6970)
Providence Children's Museum, Providence (401-273-KIDS)
Roger Williams Park Zoo, Providence (401-725-3510)

Accommodations:
AAA Jacob Hill Inn, Providence (888-336-9165)
Johnson & Wales Inn, Providence (800-232-1772)
New Yorker Motor Lodge, East Providence (401-434-8000)
State House Inn, Providence (401-351-6111)
The Cady House B&B, Providence (401-273-5398)

Jamestown (Conanicut North, Beavertail, Dutch Island)
Other Sites of Interest:
Fort Wetherill State Park, Jamestown (401-222-2632)
Jamestown Museum, Jamestown (401-423-0784)
Jamestown Windmill, Jamestown (401-423-1798)
Newport Butterfly Farm, Middletown (401-849-9519)
Newport Vineyards and Winery, Middletown (401-848-5161)

Accommodations:
Adele Turner Inn, Newport (401-847-1811)
Bay Voyage, Jamestown (401-423-2100)
Howard Johnson Inn, Middletown (401-849-2000)
Hydrangea House Inn, Newport (401-846-4435)
Meadowlark Recreational Vehicle Park, Newport (401-846-9455)

Little Compton (Sakonnet Point)
Other Sites of Interest:
Historic Fort Adams, Newport (401-841-0707)
Little Compton Historical Society, Little Compton (401-635-4035)
Newport Art Museum, Newport (401-848-8200)
The Astors' Beechwood Mansion, Newport (401-846-3772)
Wilbor House, Barn, and Quaker Meeting House, Little Compton (401-635-4035)

Accommodations:
Chase Farm B&B, Newport (401-845-9338)
Hotel Viking, Newport (401-847-3300)
Newport Marriott, Newport (401-849-1000)
Spring Street Inn, Newport (401-847-4767)
Travelodge, Newport (401-849-4700)

Newport (Castle Hill, Newport Harbor, Rose Island)
Other Sites of Interest:
America's Cup Charters, Newport (401-846-9886)
International Tennis Hall of Fame, Newport (401-849-3990)
Museum of Newport History at the Brick Market, Newport (401-841-8770)
New England Aquarium, Newport (401-849-8490)
Newport Mansion Tours, Newport (401-847-1000)

Accommodations:
Baldwin Place, Newport (401-847-3801)
The Burbank Rose, Newport (401-849-9457)
Cliffside Inn, Newport (401-847-1811)
Newport Dinner Train, Newport (401-841-8700)
Paradise Motel, Middletown (401-847-1500)

North Kingstown / Wickford (Plum Beach and Poplar Point)
Other Sites of Interest:
Casey Farm, North Kingstown (401-295-1030)
Gilbert Stuart Birthplace, North Kingstown (401-294-3001)

Quonset Aviation Museum, North Kingstown (401-294-9540)
Smith's Castle, Wickford (401-294-3521)
Wickford Village, Wickford (401-294-4867)

Accommodations:
Boat House B&B, North Kingstown (401-295-5010)
Budget Inn of North Kingstown (401-294-4888)
Crosswinds Farm B&B, North Kingstown (401-294-6168)
Haddie Pierce House, North Kingstown (401-294-7674)
Welcome Inn, North Kingstown (401-884-9153)

Portsmouth/Prudence Island (Hog Island Shoal/Sandy Point)
Other Sites of Interest:
Green Animals, Portsmouth (401-847-1000)
Greenvale Vineyards, Portsmouth (401-847-3777)
Narragansett Bay National Estuarine Sanctuary, Prudence Island (401-683-6780)
Old School House, Portsmouth (401-683-9178)

Accommodations:
Best Western Bay Point Inn & Conference Center, Portsmouth (401-683-3600)
Founder's Brook Motel and Suites, Portsmouth (401-683-1244)
Gardenview B&B, Newport (401-849-5799)
Melville Ponds Campground, Portsmouth (401-849-8212)
The Francis Malbone House, Newport (401-846-0392)

Wakefield (Gooseberry, Point Judith)
Other Sites of Interest:
Adventureland, Narragansett (401-789-0030)
Fine Arts Center Galleries, South Kingstown (401-874-2775)
Hannah Robinson Rock and Tower, South Kingstown (401-222-2632)
Historic Fayerweather House, South Kingstown (401-789-9072)
South County Museum, Narragansett (401-783-5400)

Accommodations:
Applewood Greene B&B, South Kingstown (401-789-1937)
Blueberry Cove Inn, Narragansett (401-792-9865)
Grinnell Inn, Narragansett (401-789-4340)
Holiday Inn, South Kingstown (401-789-1051)
Kagels Cottages, Narragansett (401-783-4551)

Warwick (Conimicut, Warwick)
Other Sites of Interest:
Goddard State Park, Warwick (401-884-2010)
John Waterman Arnold House, Warwick (401-467-7647)
Pawtuxet Village, Warwick (401-738-2000)
Step Stone Falls, West Greenwich (401-222-1157)
Warwick Museum of Art, Warwick (401-737-0010)

Accommodations:
Comfort Inn Airport, Warwick (401-732-0470)
Crowne Plaza Hotel at the Crossing, Warwick (401-732-6000)
The Equinox Sailing Vessel, Warwick
(401-885-1822: summer; 941-263-6099: winter)
Henry L. Johnson House B&B, Warwick (401-781-5158)
Radisson Airport Hotel, Warwick (401-739-3000)

Westerly (Watch Hill)
Other Sites of Interest:
Babcock-Smith House, Westerly (401-596-5704)
Duck Land/Water Tours, Westerly (401-596-7761)
Flying Horse Carousel, Westerly (401-348-6540)
Frosty Drew Observatory, Charlestown (401-364-9508)
Narragansett Indian Meeting House/Church (401-364-1100)

Accommodations:
Andrea Resort Hotel, Westerly (401-348-8788)
Atlantic Beach Casino Resort, Westerly (401-322-7100)
Harbour House Inn, Westerly (401-596-7500)
Sand Castle Inn, Westerly (401-596-6900)
Sandy Shore Motel and Apartments, Westerly (401-596-5616)

Bibliography

Cassinelli, Ron, "Man of Stone," *Providence Journal*, January 14, 2000.

Dunlop, Tom. "Lightship Down," *Martha's Vineyard Magazine*, September 2003.

Gomez, Cynthia. "Palmers Island Light Rekindled," *The Standard Times*, August 31, 1999.

Marcus, Jon. *Lighthouses of New England: Your Guide to the Lighthouses of Maine, New Hampshire, Vermont, Massachusetts, Rhode Island, and Connecticut.* Stillwater, Minnesota: Voyageur Press, 2001.

Scott, Judi, "Lighthouse replica to be lifted into place," *South County* (Rhode Island) *Independent*, December 30, 1999, Volume 3.

Snow, Edward Rowe. *The Lighthouses of New England, 1716–1973.* New York: Dodd, Mead, 1973.

Works Progress Administration. *Rhode Island: a Guide to the Smallest State.* American Guide Series. Boston: Houghton Mifflin Company, 1937.

General Lighthouse Websites:
American Lighthouse Foundation: www.lighthousefoundation.org
Cyberlights Lighthouse Page: www.cyberlights.com/lh
Lighthouse Depot: www.lhdepot.com
Lighthouse Friends: www.lighthousefriends.com
Lighthouse Getaway: www.lighthousegetaway.com
Lighthouse Ratings: www.lighthouseratings.com
Lighthouses: A Photographic Journey (Internet Public Library): www.ipl.org/div/light
Massachusetts Lighthouses: www.unc.edu/~rowlett/lighthouse/ma.htm
National Park Service Maritime Heritage Program Inventory of Historic Light Stations:
       www.cr.nps.gov/maritime/ltaccess.html
New England Lighthouses: A Virtual Guide: www.lighthouse.cc
Rick's Lighthouse Screensavers: www.rickslighthouses.com
Rudy and Alice's Lighthouse Page: www.rudyalicelighthouse.net
United States Coast Guard Connecticut Light Stations:
       www.uscg.mil/hq/g-cp/history/WEBLIGHTHOUSES/LHCT.html
USA Lights: www.usalights.com

Specific Lighthouse Websites:
Bass River Light: www.lighthouseinn.com
Beavertail Lighthouse History: www.riparks.com/beavertailhistory.htm
Bird Island Lighthouse: www.by-the-sea.com/birdislandlight/
Block Island North Light Fund: www.ctol.net/~rdaines/nlfund.html
Borden Flats Light: www.lizzieborden.org
Butler Flats Light: www.cuttyhunk.com

Cape Ann Light on Thacher Island: www.thacherisland.org
Duxbury Pier Light: www.buglight.org
Martha's Vineyard Lighthouses: www.marthasvineyardhistory.org
Minot's Ledge Light: www.cohassetchamber.org/pages/minot.htm
Nantucket Lighthouses: www.nantucketonline.com/Articles/beacons.shtml
Nantucket Lightship: www.nantucketlightship.com
Nauset Light: www.nausetlight.org
Plymouth Light: www.buglight.org
Race Point Lighthouse: www.racepointlighthouse.net
Rose Island Lighthouse: www.roseislandlighthouse.org

Other Sources:
www.aoml.noaa.gov/hrd/Landsea/deadly/Table3A.htm

www.architecture.about.com/library/bl-artmoderne.htm

www.bartleby.com/310/2/2.html

www.ci.new-bedford.ma.us/governmt/MAYOR/Millennium/2000_02.htm

www.dos.state.ny.us/cstl/Final_Draft_HTML/Tech_Report_HTM/Land_Use/
Hist_Dev_Patterns/Prime_HDP.htm

www.experts.longisland.com/lighthouses/archive_article.php?ExpArtID=1089

www.lighthousefoundation.org/creaaddress.cfm

www.starvingwriters.org/eThis/Fiction/Mystery/April/ghost2.html

www.uscgaux.org/~01311/Nobska.htm

Notes